TWAYNE'S WORLD AUTHORS SERIES

A Survey of the World's Literature

RUSSIA

Charles A. Moser, George Washington University

EDITOR

Denis Fonvizin

TWAS 560

DENIS FONVIZIN

By CHARLES A. MOSER
George Washington University

TWAYNE PUBLISHERS
A DIVISION OF G. K. HALL & CO., BOSTON

Copyright © 1979 by G.K. Hall & Co.

Published in 1979 by Twayne Publishers,
A Division of G.K. Hall & Co.
All Rights Reserved

Printed on permanent/durable acid-free paper and bound
in the united States of America

First Printing

Library of Congress Cataloging in Publication Data

Moser, Charles A
Denis Fonvizin.

(Twayne's world authors series ; TWAS 560 : Russia)
Bibliography: p. 144 - 46
Includes index.
1. Fonvizin, Denis Ivanovich, 1745-1792—Criticism
and interpretation.
PG3313.F6Z78   891.7'2'2   78-27127
ISBN 0-8057-6402-X

Contents

About the Author

Charles A. Moser was born in Knoxville, Tennessee, and took his undergraduate degree at Yale. After taking his graduate degrees at Columbia (with a year of work at Leningrad State University), he taught at Yale from 1960 to 1967 in Slavic languages. In 1967 he came to the George Washington University in Washington, D.C., where he is currently Professor of Slavic. He served as Chairman of the Department of Slavic Languages from 1969 to 1974, and has been editor of the Russian section of the Twayne's World Authors Series since 1975.

Moser's principal interests are the history of Russian literature, particularly of the 1860's; and Bulgarian literature, particularly of the first four decades of the twentieth century. He is the author of a number of articles and reviews in these fields, and of the following books: *Antinihilism in the Russian Novel of the 1860's* (1964), *Pisemsky: A Provincial Realist* (1969), *A History of Bulgarian Literature 865-1944* (1972), and *Ivan Turgenev* (1972).

Preface

"Freedom's friend," Pushkin called him admiringly, in *Eugene Onegin*. For the greatest poet of nineteenth-century Russia, Fonvizin was a kindred soul, one who represented the best in the literary life of a glittering period of the Russian empire.

Since Pushkin's time, Fonvizin's reputation has fluctuated in Russia. Though honored with one of the first serious studies of an eighteenth-century writer to be done in the nineteenth century—that by Prince Petr Vyazemsky published in 1848—he has aroused a certain animosity in his biographers. Vyazemsky denigrated Fonvizin's originality and took issue with him on a number of points, thus initiating something of a tradition in Fonvizin scholarship which continued in Russia until the Soviet period and still exists to a degree in the West. If books have their fates, so perhaps do authors.

Until recently there has been little Western scholarship on Fonvizin at all. In 1976 Alexis Strycek published a close study, done in the best French tradition, in Paris, but before that time there existed virtually no separate works on Fonvizin in Western languages with the exception of an obscure study of 1935 by Leone Savoj in Italian, which was so inaccessible that even the encyclopedic Strycek failed to note it. An occasional article on him appeared in French or Italian, but in English there was almost no secondary work on him until 1973, when Marvin Kantor published an article on *The Brigadier*, a preliminary to his book of 1974 containing translations of all Fonvizin's plays prefaced by a general study of his life and work. Until the present time, articles on Fonvizin in English have been few and far between, although English-language surveys of Russian literature pay him proper attention, and many of his writings, including especially his masterpiece *The Minor*, have been translated into English, sometimes more than once. But on the whole Fonvizin has been neglected in Western scholarship, although—following a certain hiatus after 1917—since the Second World War a number of Soviet scholars have published books on him, invariably favorable in their interpretation.

The present volume is the first introductory book on Fonvizin's life and work in English. After the initial biographical chapter, my approach varies according to the nature of the material discussed in each chapter. Fonvizin's major works—*The Brigadier, The Minor,* and the travel letters—are treated separately in individual chapters from the literary and historical point of view. But his translation work of the 1760s, before he published his first important original work, is presented in the context of the literary trends of that decade, quite a seminal one in the history of eighteenth-century Russian literature. The sixth chapter, on "Literature and Politics," deals with the political ideas, implicit and explicit, in his work of the 1780s: during all his life Fonvizin was associated with politics, politicians, and statesmen as well as literature, and he always believed literature should deal with the social and moral issues of the day. Finally, I have added a short chapter on Fonvizin's contribution to the development of the Russian literary language, and another outlining his living influence on subsequent Russian literature. Throughout the book I have sought to direct the reader to the most valuable secondary works extant for further reading on particular topics in Fonvizin's life and work.

I hope, then, that this brief volume will serve as a convenient introduction for the English-speaking student to the literary accomplishments of Denis Fonvizin and his intellectual contributions to Russian culture. I hope too that some of the more general questions which I have occasionally raised in connection with his career may be of interest to specialists in eighteenth-century Russian intellectual history, even though this book cannot pretend to match the detail of some existing studies of Fonvizin.

At this point I must express my appreciation to the George Washington University, which provided me the sabbatical semester I needed to write this book; and to the Kennan Institute for Advanced Russian Studies of the Smithsonian Institution in Washington, D.C., for granting me a fellowship over that same period which provided access to the working facilities which I required. Neither of these institutions bears the slightest responsibility for the materials and conclusions offered in this volume.

Chronology

1788   Plans to issue a journal with his writings, *The Friend of Honest Men, or Starodum,* but is refused permission. Hopes to publish his collected works, but is unable to see the project through.

1789   Summer: visits the baths at Baldone and Mitau for his health.

1790– Writes *The Selection of a Tutor* and *An Open-Hearted Confes-*
1791? *sion.*

1792   December 1: dies in St. Petersburg, after an evening spent at the home of the poet Gavriil Derzhavin.

CHAPTER 1

Biography

I Childhood and Youth, 1745–62

THOUGH it might not seem so, Fonvizin is a Russian name. At least Alexander Pushkin argued that it was in defending the form "Fonvizin" against the semi-Russified Germanic "Fon-Vizin" which the writer himself used during his lifetime.[1] Pushkin maintained that Fonvizin was "the most Russian of all Russians," and from that it logically followed that Russians should insist on writing his name in the Russian manner. If Pushkin did not entirely carry the day in the nineteenth century, in the course of the twentieth the form "Fonvizin" has become standard in Soviet and Western treatments of this outstanding eighteenth-century literary figure. And it is right that this should be so, since Denis Fonvizin never considered himself anything but Russian, and had to study German in school. By the time of his birth, his family had become entirely Russified, at a great remove from their ancestors, who apparently first entered service under Ivan the Terrible in the mid-sixteenth century and rose to prominence in Russian affairs approximately a century later, under Tsar Alexey Mikhaylovich.

Denis's father, Ivan Andreevich Fonvizin (1705–86), was not especially distinguished in the eyes of the world. He was a civil servant residing in a not especially fashionable section of Moscow. But as his son saw him, he was an exemplary man and parent. In his unfinished autobiography written at the conclusion of his life, Fonvizin recalled him as a totally honorable individual, one who would neither solicit favors from those more highly placed than he nor exact them from those over whom he exercised some temporary authority. He led an exemplary "Christian life," Fonvizin wrote: he neither drank nor overate, he did not waste his substance at cards, and though married twice, he remained invariably faithful to his wife. Indeed, he did so under very unusual circumstances: when his

brother became hopelessly entangled in debt, Ivan consented to
marry an elderly widow who had fallen in love with him and was
willing to retire his brother's debts. At the age of eighteen, Ivan
married the lady and cared for her faithfully for the remaining twelve
years of her life.[2] Only after her death did Ivan Fonvizin marry a
younger woman, Ekaterina Vasilievna Dmitrieva-Mamonova, the
daughter of an admiral and descendant of an ancient noble family.
Fonvizin rather conventionally described her as a "virtuous wife,
loving mother, intelligent homemaker, and magnanimous supervisor
of servants [gospozha]" (II, 84). Evidently she exercised a lesser
influence over Denis than did his father.

In time Ekaterina Vasilievna bore her husband eight children, with
six of them arriving at single-year intervals between 1744 and 1749,
and two others coming later, in 1756 and 1760. In his autobiography,
Fonvizin gave his father much credit for managing to raise and
educate eight children without going into debt (II, 83). Fonvizin
himself later emphatically failed to meet that standard even though
he had no children at all.

Only two of Fonvizin's siblings deserve more detailed mention
here. His sister Feodosiya, his elder by one year, shared his literary
and intellectual interests. They were very close, and when Denis
moved to St. Petersburg in the 1760s, she became his most valued
correspondent and confidante. Fonvizin's younger brother Pavel
(1746–1803) became a man of some distinction. He had literary
aspirations and did some translating, eventually rising to become a
member of the Senate and Director of Moscow University from 1784
to 1796. The surviving documents, however, make it appear that
Pavel was never so close to Denis as was Feodosiya.

The exact date of Denis Fonvizin's birth is a matter of scholarly
dispute.[3] The inscription upon his gravestone indicates that he died
at the age of forty-eight, which would mean that he was born in 1744,
since he died in 1792. However, the church records of his parish show
that in 1751 he was six years old, and a birth date of 1745 locates him
neatly among his brothers and sisters in the series of annual births
from 1744 to 1749. In his autobiography Fonvizin mentions that he
was no more than fourteen when he made his first trip from Moscow
to St. Petersburg, which apparently took place in 1759. A piece of
indirect evidence on this question—so far as I know overlooked until
now—is to be found in his later work *Povestvovanie mnimogo
glukhogo i nemogo* (Tale of a Pretended Deaf-Mute), in which the
narrator says he was seventeen at the time of a journey in 1762 (II,

19). On the other hand, a church record of 1768 indicates that in that year Fonvizin was twenty-four years of age, which supports the witness of the inscription upon his gravestone. Still, the general consensus now is that he was born on April 3, 1745—although it is possible that he was in fact born a year earlier.

However that may be, the young Denis seems to have had a reasonably happy childhood. One scholar has attributed some importance to the fact that apparently he had no foreign tutors at home.[4] In fact, Fonvizin tells us little about his childhood education, and what he does say indicates that his parents were responsible for most of that. He began to receive formal schooling, he recalled, at the age of four (II, 84).

Fonvizin also mentioned some character traits rooted in his childhood. One was a tendency to lose his temper. Although it is unclear how he knew of this, he reports that he was weaned very late, at the age of three. When he was finally deprived of his mother's breast, he flew into an infantile rage, and told his father that he "would have liked to ram both you and myself into the ground" (II, 84). That temper stayed with him all his life, although he himself believed that he was essentially a good-hearted sort. Then too, an aesthetic feeling seems to have been aroused in him quite early. He remembered that his aunt used to visit them frequently, occasionally bringing them playing cards with red backs as presents. The young Denis was so taken with the cards that he concocted all sorts of childishly devious devices to obtain more of them (II, 85). This experience taught him that it is ordinarily better to be straightforward in one's desires: he needed only to tell his aunt directly that he wanted more of the cards. But the episode also shows that his love for beautiful things was inborn in him. Beauty attracted him from the beginning.

Denis's early education ended about 1755, when Moscow University opened its doors. This, the first university in Russia, came into being through the efforts of the great poet, scholar, and scientist Mikhail Lomonosov, who provided theoretical guidance, and the statesman Ivan Shuvalov, who guided the project through at the highest levels and persuaded the Empress Elizabeth to decree the institution's establishment. Today the university is named in honor of Lomonosov, who, as Pushkin once wrote, "*was* our first university."

Such a large enterprise could not be begun without some birth-pangs. For one thing, the state of Russian secondary education was such that there were few students qualified to enter the university,

and so it was provided from the start with a preparatory school. At
first little distinction was made between the preparatory school and
the university itself, which explains how Fonvizin could enter the
university at the age of ten to pursue a curriculum which included
Latin and German, languages which he was to put to quite practical
use in a few years.

Moscow University experienced difficulties in recruiting qualified
professors as well as qualified students. In his autobiography Fonvizin recounts some amusing stories illustrating the low level of
instruction at the institution in its first years. In preparing his pupils
for an examination in Latin, for instance, their instructor resorted to
ingenious cheating to insure that they did well in the eyes of the
outside examiner: after all, his reputation was at stake also. The
instructor wore a coat with five buttons and a vest with four buttons.
The five coat buttons represented the five declensions, the four vest
buttons the four conjugations: when the examiner asked about
declensions and conjugations, the instructor would grasp the appropriate button to indicate the correct answer to the student (II, 87–88).
Fonvizin hastened to add, however, that the quality of instruction at
his *alma mater* had improved substantially since his time within its
walls.

For the Moscow University of that time, Fonvizin was an excellent
student. His name appeared consistently in lists, published in the
local Moscow newspaper, of outstanding students, and he received
several medals for scholastic excellence. In his autobiography,
though, he described the circumstances under which he had won
such a medal in geography. When the examiners asked into which sea
the Volga River emptied, one student claimed it was the Black Sea,
and another the White Sea. But Fonvizin candidly admitted that he
did not know, whereupon the examiners unanimously granted him
the geography award. Fonvizin remarked that perhaps he deserved a
medal for practical ethics, but hardly for geography in that instance
(II, 88). Still, despite all its shortcomings, Moscow University gave
Fonvizin a great deal, he thought, including most especially a "taste
for literature" (II, 88). His years there were far from wasted.

Scholarship also had its more immediate rewards, as Fonvizin was
to discover. Apparently in the winter of 1758–59, the Director of the
university arranged a trip to St. Petersburg in order to exhibit some of
the first fruits of the first Russian university to the Court and to Count
Shuvalov. Denis and his brother Pavel were selected for the journey
to the capital, where they stayed with an uncle. After a few days the

group met with Shuvalov, who evidently was willing to give credit where credit was due: he introduced the young students to the "immortal" Lomonosov, as Fonvizin termed him. Upon learning that they were students of Latin, Lomonosov delivered an extemporaneous discourse on the importance of that language. Quite possibly this was the first occasion on which Denis made the acquaintance of an established and famous literary figure.

The St. Petersburg trip was memorable for other reasons as well. Although the youngsters did not meet Elizabeth then, the magnificence of the Russian Court, with its "gold gleaming everywhere, its collection of people with blue and red ribbons of distinction, its multitude of beautiful ladies, and then its enormous music" (II, 92), deeply impressed Fonvizin's childish mind. The aesthetic leitmotif of this description is noteworthy: although later Fonvizin came to understand what lay behind the Court, on the surface it seemed to embody taste and beauty.

Perhaps even more than the Court, the St. Petersburg theater, then in its infancy, made a lasting impression on Fonvizin. He had never attended the theater in Moscow, and so the visit to the St. Petersburg theater came as a revelation to him. Later on he realized that the play he saw that day was rather banal, but to the boy at the time it seemed a "work of the greatest intellect," so humorous as to cause him to dissolve in cascades of mirth. He soon discovered that a number of St. Petersburg actors frequented his uncle's house, where he first met the comic actor Yakov Shumsky; the founder of the Russian theater, Fedor Volkov; and also one of the greatest figures in the history of the eighteenth-century Russian theater, the actor Ivan Dmitrevsky (1736–97), who later became a very close friend of Fonvizin's (II, 92–93). In such fashion did Fonvizin enter upon a lifelong infatuation with the theater and the people of the theater.

After the fabulous world of the capital, Moscow must have seemed a trifle prosaic, although Denis was very attached to his family and hated to be parted from it. He devoted himself to his studies once again. He had some excellent instructors, including especially Johann Schaden, a teacher of philosophy with whom he studied logic. During his visit to St. Petersburg, a young nobleman whom Fonvizin found very impressive had twitted him with his ignorance of French, so upon returning to Moscow Denis set about learning that language properly, and discovered that his Latin was of considerable assistance in doing so. Two years later he could read Voltaire in the original with a little difficulty (II, 93–94).

At about this time the future literary man first tried his hand at literary translation. He began with the German version of a lengthy work by Jean Terrasson, *Geroiskaia dobrodetel', ili zhizn' Sifa* (Heroic Virtue, or the Life of Sethos, originally published in French anonymously as *Séthos, histoire, ou Vie privée tirée des documens anecdotes de l'ancienne Egypte, traduite d'un manuscrit grec*). When his French improved, he shifted to translating from the original instead of the German rendering. The four volumes of the translation appeared over the years between 1762 and 1768.

Fonvizin's first major publication, however, came out even earlier, in 1761, when he was scarcely more than sixteen. At the suggestion of a publisher and bookseller, Fonvizin undertook the translation from the German of fables by Ludvig Holberg (1684–1754), one of the founders of modern Danish literature. Entitled *Basni nravouchitel' nye s iz"iasneniiami* (Fables and Morals), the book included some 225 of Holberg's brief prose fables equipped with short morals spelling out the moral stance the reader should adopt toward their subject matter.

Unfortunately, the bookseller was not so moral a character as Holberg. He promised Fonvizin for his labors fifty rubles' worth of foreign editions, an offer which the young student happily accepted. But when the books arrived, they turned out to be pornographic in content. Those volumes, he recalled, "corrupted my imagination and disoriented my soul" (II, 89). In view of the fact—mentioned in his autobiography—that he had difficulty in controlling his passions anyway, these books impelled him to attempt putting theory into practice with a girl of his age who was both stupid and unlovely, whose only attraction was her sex. Fonvizin prepared the groundwork by showing the girl the same books which had infected him, but he could go little further for a terribly mundane reason: the doors in her house were so poorly made that they could never be entirely closed, and thus the two of them could find no privacy. Under the circumstances, Denis soon tired of his companion and departed the scene (II, 88–89). But he never forgot the damage which those books had inflicted upon his moral standards.

With the passage of time came changes at the highest level of the state. The year 1762 was a critical one for Russia, and also for Fonvizin personally. In 1761 the Empress Elizabeth died, to be very briefly succeeded by Peter III. Peter's policies, however, were so unacceptable to the highest nobility that in late June of 1762, after he had been on the throne for some six months, he was removed by a coup and later murdered. His place was taken by his wife, Catherine, originally a German princess, who entered upon a reign which would last until 1796 and see the Russian Empire attain the zenith of its power and influence. Fonvizin would spend his entire adult life under Catherine's reign.

By 1762, however, Fonvizin was still only seventeen. Although he was officially still in the military, he felt no attraction for a military career. Thus, when the Court arrived in Moscow for the coronation of September 1762, Fonvizin came to the attention of Vice-Chancellor Alexander Golitsyn, who arranged for him to be employed by the Foreign Office *(Kollegiia inostrannykh del)* as a translator. His service petition of the time (II, 609–10) makes it appear that he received formal approval for the appointment from Catherine sometime in October 1762. Evidently he performed his duties quite satisfactorily, for, he recalls, the Chancellor gave him very important diplomatic papers to translate (II, 94). Moreover, despite his tender years, in December of 1762 he carried out the minor diplomatic mission of delivering a decoration to the Countess of Mecklenburg-Schwerin. He fulfilled his task in January of 1763 (travel was a slow process in those days) and felt he had made a good impression both at home and abroad (II, 94).

Denis Fonvizin's formal education was now ended. He had embarked upon the literary and political course which he was to follow for the rest of his life, as he moved toward the superficial glitter of the Court which had so overwhelmed him a few short years before.

II   *St. Petersburg and the Beginnings of a Literary Career,*
1762–69

Fonvizin did not move to the capital immediately, since the Court remained in Moscow for several months in 1762–63 for the festivities surrounding Catherine's coronation. Prominent among them was the splendid pageant entitled "Victorious Minerva," whose organizer, Fedor Volkov—Fonvizin had met him in St. Petersburg—literally caught his death of cold while supervising it. Upon returning from his German mission, Fonvizin evidently worked at his official translating while living at home, but when the Court removed to St. Petersburg in the summer of 1763, he followed it to the capital.

At about this point Fonvizin enjoyed the political and literary patronage of Ivan Perfilevich Elagin (1725–96), a prominent statesman with literary pretensions. Elagin had been a supporter of

Catherine in the 1750s, before it was quite safe to be such, and after Catherine came to the throne he acquired some substantial powers. Thus in 1766 he took charge of the development of the state theaters. From about 1763 to 1769 Fonvizin worked as Elagin's assistant. He was disappointed, though, in his hopes that Elagin would assist him in advancing his political or literary career.

Evidently there were reasons for Elagin's failure to promote the fortunes of his protégé. One of them was another assistant, Vladimir Lukin (1737–94), a playwright of some reputation in the 1760s. Lukin and Elagin had collaborated in the translation of a lengthy French novel into Russian, published between 1756 and 1764. Their literary and personal relationship was apparently close and of long standing, and of course antedated the relationship between Fonvizin and Elagin. Lukin evidently did not care for Fonvizin as a competitor either in the civil service or in literature, and Fonvizin fully reciprocated his distaste. In 1766, for instance, Fonvizin told his parents that Elagin supposedly now recognized his mistake in promoting a man like Lukin, whose family had "never had any ranks and who were born to serve and not to rule." "You can't imagine," he went on, "all the malice, all the dirty intrigues which he has employed to damage me in the eyes of Ivan Perfilevich [Elagin] and his entire family."[5] In his autobiography Fonvizin characterized Lukin as a person of "limitless conceit and unbearably difficult character" (II, 95), who took an instant dislike to him for some unknown reason. It is quite possible, given the snobbishness of his description of Lukin as "born to serve and not to rule," that social pride had much to do with the hostility between the two writers. In all likelihood Fonvizin did not agree with Lukin on many matters and was quick to voice his disagreement. And since Lukin had greater continuing influence with Elagin than did Fonvizin, Fonvizin's position was always uncomfortable, and finally became untenable. Still, during much of his service with Elagin he seems to have enjoyed a very personal relationship with his chief; he accompanied him wherever he happened to be, stayed in his house on occasion, and seems to have been treated as though he were a member of the Elagin family.

Not much of Fonvizin's correspondence from the 1760s has been preserved; what there is deals more with personal and literary matters than with Fonvizin's official duties. In a letter of 1764 he does mention his participation in an official ceremony when the Polish ambassador arrived to present his credentials to Vice-Chancellor

Golitsyn: Fonvizin received the ambassador at the entrance, and remained to converse with his party during his audience with the Vice-Chancellor (II, 333).

On the whole Fonvizin's official duties were not overly arduous during the 1760s, and he had sufficient time to attend to literary matters. Literarily speaking, the transitional 1760s witnessed a shift from the predominance of poetry to the rise of prose. Fonvizin is now primarily remembered as a prose writer, and correctly so, but he was not devoid of poetic talent and for a time in the 1760s considered working extensively in poetry. Such an inclination might have been reinforced by the fact that the greatest of Neoclassical Russian odists, Lomonosov, died only in 1765. On December 13, 1763, Fonvizin enclosed two odes in a letter to his sister (II, 326); a short time later he wrote to her that he felt like writing something in verse (II, 330). Indeed at about this time he was working on a verse translation of Voltaire's *Alzire*. He never published it, however, and later on spoke slightingly of it as a "sin of my youth" (II, 94). Since there were no Russian literary critics to speak of in existence then, Fonvizin had to depend upon his own intuition in evaluating his poetic abilities. That intuition told him his talents in this area were minimal, and consequently we now possess not a single ode from the period of Fonvizin's youth, and rather few works in verse of any kind.

One of his better long attempts at a verse work was a translation and adaptation of J. P. Gresset's play *Sidnei*, done in 1764 and published under the Russian title *Korion*. This work is rendered in rather pleasant verse, and shows that in fact Fonvizin did have some abilities along these lines. In the end, however, the work proved to be a turn down an artistic blind alley, not just because it was in verse, but because it was a travesty, a tragedy transformed into a comedy. Travesty was certainly in literary fashion just then, and he could have continued along that path had he wished. In a letter of August 1763 to his sister, Fonvizin reports having purchased an edition of Paul Scarron, the most outstanding French travesty-writer, who, he said, was considered a "glorious jester" (II, 319). In the end Fonvizin did not resort to travesty to combat a superannuated Neoclassicism.

Although Fonvizin did some important original writing during the 1760s, most of his attention was concentrated upon translation. In 1762 he had contributed to a quarterly journal entitled *Sobranie luchshikh sochinenii* (Collection of the Best Works), published by a Moscow University professor, Johann Reichel. Fonvizin produced a number of brief translations for it. In addition, he began or continued translating several longer works, both literary and political in nature. Thus he continued work on Terrasson's *Séthos* until it was completed in 1768; in 1763 he translated a short novel by Jean-Jacques Barthélémy, *Les Amours de Carite et Polydore*, under the title *Liubov' Karity i Polidora* (The Love of Carita and Polydore). In 1766 Fonvizin came out with a translation in quite a different area, this time Gabriel-François Coyer's *La Noblesse commercante*, rendered under the title *Torguiushchee dvorianstvo* (The Commercial Nobility).

At the end of the decade, in 1769, Fonvizin returned to the publishers' lists with literary translations of François-Thomas Baculard d'Arnaud's *Sidney et Silli, ou La Bienfaisance et la Reconnaissance* under a title which was an exact translation; and of Paul-Jérémie Bitaube's *Joseph*, a Sentimental work based upon the biblical story of Joseph and his brothers.

All in all, Fonvizin produced an impressive quantity of translations during the 1760s. During the later 1770s he published a few more translations, and even in the 1780s they had not entirely disappeared from his repertory, but when he announced plans for a journal in 1788, he explicitly stipulated that it would contain no translations.[6]

If Fonvizin's letters of the 1760s provide little information on his official duties, they afford considerable insight into his character. In particular, his letters to his sister Feodosiya, though not numerous, open a window into the writer's emotional life during his formative period.

Immediately after moving to the northern capital, Fonvizin felt isolated, lonely, and friendless. In August of 1763 he wrote his sister that he had no acquaintances: he did not associate with the cadets at the military academy because he lacked sympathy for the military mind, and he had little to do with the Academy of Sciences because nearly everyone there was a "pedant," or so he thought. "You can understand," he told her with exaggerated pathos, "that it is very difficult for a person with a sensitive heart to live in society!" (II, 318–19). His feelings of isolation at this point were mostly temporary, though, for he was not one to languish at home. Even in 1763 he participated in a busy round of social activities. For instance, in December he wrote his sister that he had been to the theater to see Sumarokov's play *Sinav* (II, 327). His letters from the end of 1763 describe—sometimes in great detail—his visits to the theater, attendance at masked balls, lunches and dinners with other interesting guests at the homes of various individuals. In short, the superficial observer at the time might well have concluded that Fonvizin had found his place in St. Petersburg society rather quickly and easily. And yet, in the midst of the social round, Fonvizin consistently felt that he was an "outsider" *(chuzhestranets)*, even after he had lived in St. Petersburg for several years. A passage from a letter of early 1766 to his sister sums up his psychological state at the time:

> On Friday I had dinner at P. M. Kheraskov's, and then went to a masquerade. There was a tremendous throng of people there, but I swear to you that all the same it was as if I had been in the wilderness. There was hardly a single person there with whom I could converse and obtain any satisfaction at all. (II, 337)

The cause of Fonvizin's disenchantment with society was his feeling of intellectual superiority to those around him. This attitude emerges with striking clarity in another passage from the same letter of 1766 in which he describes an encounter with a lady of his acquaintance at the theater. She had not been very friendly toward him, and Fonvizin had reacted accordingly:

> Without flattering her, I can say that during the twenty-nine days I've been away, she has become so much more stupid that she surpasses any animal you can think of. . . . I thought it advisable not to remain in their box any longer so as not to play some prank, since no one can do anything intelligent when he is dealing with fools. (II, 338)

This attitude remained consistent in Fonvizin's view of St. Petersburg. In June of 1768 he wrote to his parents that he was constantly disgusted by the hypocrisy of society. "I am completely and utterly repelled," he wrote, "by all the trivialities in which society people today find their chief satisfaction" (II, 348). And in 1770 he confided to his sister that he sought to lose himself in the whirl of the social round because he found existence in Court circles so boring and unrewarding (II, 351).

The emptyheadedness and stupidity with which Fonvizin was surrounded engendered several reactions within him. One was irritation pure and simple: he nursed resentments against those with whom he had to associate. Sometimes he realized that he was himself partly at fault, as, for instance, when he wrote his sister in 1766 that he had become entirely unbearable to be with although before he had been quite "merry." "The very things which used to amuse me," he said, "now throw me into a rage" (II, 336). More frequently, however, he adopted the view that he was himself an "honest man" (*chestnyi chelovek*)—the phrase cropped up continually in his writings all through his life—surrounded by people morally far below him. He spoke thus of Lukin in 1766, when he told his parents that his bureaucratic associate was a "good-for-nothing" (*bezdel'nik*), whereas he, Fonvizin, was an "honest man" (II, 343). Moreover, Fonvizin had a way of not confining his opinions to personal letters to his family. Indeed he became renowned (not always in a positive sense) in St. Petersburg society for the sharpness of his tongue and the agility of his wit. Fonvizin himself later regretted his conceit, but some of his contemporaries did not forget it. One such person was the obscure poet Alexander Khvostov (1753–1820). In a satirical poem attacking Fonvizin dating from about 1780, Khvostov maintained that a good *bon mot* is not invariably the product of a fine mind, that "fools" can sometimes strike them off as well.[7] And we have documents to show that Fonvizin could be unduly sharp with his intellectual opponents when he wished.

Fonvizin attempted to mitigate his loneliness by seeking feminine companionship. This was particularly the case when he had first arrived in St. Petersburg and, we should recall, had not yet reached the age of twenty. At some point in late 1763 or early 1764 he told his sister that he could find no "object" for his affections in the capital (II, 319), adding that he had heard from other sources that since his departure "beautiful Amazons" had appeared in Moscow, who rode about the streets on horseback making conquests with "glances" (II, 320). In one or two other letters of about the same time Fonvizin lets his sister know that he has failed to find a kindred soul among the young ladies of St. Petersburg.

Thereafter we hear little of Fonvizin and women until about 1769, when he spent several months in Moscow doing some writing and met a certain married woman who, he recalled in his autobiography, captivated him by the qualities of her mind and soul. He felt nothing but esteem for her, and evidently the affair remained platonic, since, as he phrased it, "my passion was based on respect and did not depend on the difference in our sexes" (II, 96): such had definitely not been the case with the girl whom he thought to seduce some years earlier. When about to return to St. Petersburg, Fonvizin made an avowal to her and learned that he was loved as well. He preferred, however, simply to cherish this love in his heart.

But if Fonvizin was for long unsuccessful in finding a mate, he managed to aid his sister in this regard. Upon his arrival in St. Petersburg he had become a close friend to Vasily Argamakov, the son of the Director of Moscow University. Fonvizin found Argamakov a person of "enlightened intellect" (II, 330), the sort who could truly share his interests, and he became what Fonvizin termed the "witness of my life" (II, 330) during the final months of 1763. Then Argamakov decided to move to Moscow, and on January 28, 1764, Fonvizin wrote a long and warm letter of recommendation for him to his sister (II, 330–32). The journey from St. Petersburg to Moscow in those times took several days, and mail delivery was correspondingly slow. Therefore, after arriving in Moscow and meeting Feodosiya, Argamakov must have proposed to her within a few days, for on February 21 Fonvizin received word of his proposal. Fonvizin wrote to his sister the next day, giving his blessing and backing to the proposed match, which he had hoped for all along (II, 333–35). The couple were married toward the end of 1764 and apparently were happy enough, although Argamakov did not always prove to be the most skillful of providers for his family.

Argamakov was not Fonvizin's only close associate in the St. Petersburg of the 1760s. Another good friend for several years was Prince Fedor Kozlovsky, who fell at the battle of Chesme in 1770. A graduate of Moscow University, he shared many of Fonvizin's intellectual and literary interests, although unfortunately his influence was not always beneficial. In his autobiography Fonvizin blamed Kozlovsky for nurturing philosophical and religious doubts within him, for encouraging him in atheism and blasphemy which he could not recall "without horror" at the end of his life (II, 95). His youthful inexperience and satirical bent led him to join in blasphemous conversations and to compose one or two mildly skeptical works—especially the "Poslanie k slugam moim" (Epistle to My Servants, probably written in the mid-1760s)—which he later regretted having composed.

Aside from such personal relationships as these, we may assume, despite the dearth of direct evidence in the available documentation, that Fonvizin from time to time encountered the leading writers of the day in capital society. These included the outstanding playwright of the time, Alexander Sumarokov, of whom Fonvizin used to do impersonations (II, 99); the indefatigable translator but not especially gifted poet Vasily Trediakovsky; and the eminent Masonic intellectual and future author of the Russian Neoclassical epic poem *Ros-*

siada, Mikhail Kheraskov (in a letter of 1770 to his sister, Fonvizin remarked that Kheraskov was usually drunk, while his wife managed rarely to be at home [II, 351]). Since the number of prominent Russian writers of the day was small, Fonvizin must have had at least a passing acquaintance with a considerable fraction of them.

Literary and personal linkages were conjoined in Fonvizin's relationships with Elagin and Lukin. The battle for influence over Elagin between the two assistants went sometimes better, sometimes worse, but in the long run Lukin prevailed over Fonvizin. In mid-1766, for example, Fonvizin was in Peterhof with Elagin and his family, his situation temporarily improved. At that time Fonvizin praised Ivan Perfilevich for his "intellect enlightened with knowledge," his good heart, his patriotism; in fact, Fonvizin went so far as to speak of him as an "honest man," and accounted himself fortunate to be serving under such a superior (II, 343). But this state of things did not endure. Very likely Fonvizin's absence in Moscow for about a year in 1767 allowed Lukin to weaken his position somewhat, although not completely, since by April of 1768 Fonvizin was visiting Tsarskoe Selo with Elagin. However, he reported in July that Elagin's liking for him seemed no more than personal: his superior was unwilling to recommend a promotion for him, and so Fonvizin had arrived at a dead end in his career (II, 347). Realizing the hopelessness of his situation, by September Fonvizin had decided to seek a release from his position with Elagin, to whom by now he referred, quite unflatteringly, as a "freak" *(urod)* (II, 349–50). The politics of government service, however, was such that it would be difficult for Fonvizin to locate another position immediately after leaving Elagin's employ. Consequently, he loosened the ties between them gradually by requesting another leave of absence, and spent some six months in Moscow during 1769.

He put his Moscow time to good use, for the year 1769 saw the publication of one of his longest literary translations, *Joseph,* as well as the shorter *Sidney and Silli.* In fact, 1769 was an important year for Fonvizin and for Russian literature generally. In that year Fonvizin completed his first original play, *Brigadir* (The Brigadier), and in December he left Elagin's service and began work as a secretary to Count Nikita Panin (1718–83), one of the most powerful figures at Catherine's court. In Panin Fonvizin would find his ideal of statesman and political thinker, and to him he would dedicate his political energies so long as Panin lived.

III *Political Eminence and European Traveler, 1769–82*

Fonvizin could not have known it, but Panin's star was already on the wane by 1769. We learn from Fonvizin's correspondence that he had struck up an acquaintance with some of Panin's assistants at least by 1766 (II, 344). It is uncertain whether he knew Panin himself in 1766, although they were acquainted by the time he wrote *The Brigadier*, and Panin gave him the encouragement and assistance which Elagin would not provide. Fonvizin was rightly gratified by such attention.

Count Nikita Panin was heavily influenced in his thinking by the political ideals behind the reforms of Peter the Great.[8] He achieved political prominence for his conduct of a responsible mission to Sweden which lasted from 1748 to 1760, when he protected Russia's interests in a potentially hostile rival kingdom. His most important state appointment came in 1759–60, when he was picked as tutor to Catherine's son, the future Paul I. He derived most of his authority from this position, which he retained until Paul reached his majority. For not only did this post give Panin direct access to the Empress herself, it also provided him the exciting opportunity to inculcate in a future monarch those moral principles by which an ideal ruler ought to be guided. And Panin set out carefully and judiciously to achieve this latter aim, and also to ensure that Paul actually came to the throne. The latter objective caused tension between him and Catherine, who had no intention of handing over the throne to her son. Panin did not live to see Paul in power, and it is just as well, for he would have been grievously disappointed in the practical results of his attempts at education.

In 1760, however, Paul was still very young; Panin was a convinced supporter of Catherine and an opponent of Peter III. Panin was deeply involved in the coup against Peter III, and it was he who received Peter's abdication. Although he had wanted Paul to succeed to the throne immediately, he made his peace with Catherine's accession, and soon became a principal, though unofficial, personal advisor to her.

Panin and his allies in the upper reaches of the state bureaucracy embraced certain political ideals which they hoped to implement. To achieve their aims they acted in many ways as a "party," as David Ransel has shown. But they were not the only party at Court, and Catherine was intelligent enough to realize that she could not accept in its entirety the program of any one "party" lest she become simply its tool, and alienate others whom she also needed in order to rule. Even an autocrat of all the Russias could not issue commands into the void: they had to be carried out by people, people such as those who made up the "Panin party," whose allegiance she had to retain.

If immediately after the coup of 1762, as David Ransel writes, Panin "for all practical purposes . . . functioned as the chancellor of state,"[9] by the summer of 1763, after Catherine's partial rejection of his project for introducing the seeds of a constitutional order into Russia, the Panin party's fortunes were at a low ebb. But a winning struggle over foreign policy soon restored those fortunes.

The other chief faction at Court—aside from the Orlov faction, which was primarily a personal one based upon the circumstance that Grigory Orlov was Catherine's lover at the time—was the Bestuzhev party, grouped about Aleksey Bestuzhev. The Bestuzhev party sought a pro-Austrian policy aimed against Prussia, whereas the Panin group advocated the "Northern Accord," which would ally Russia with Prussia and Denmark against the Hapsburg-Bourbon system. When Catherine chose to follow the Panin foreign policy, by the fall of 1763 Panin was once more in the ascendant, and indeed took charge of most Russian foreign relations for several years, down to the point when the outbreak of war with Turkey in December of 1768 signified the failure of his policy. The outbreak of the war was also instrumental in terminating the work of the famous commission for the codification of the laws which Catherine convened in 1767–68, and which gave Russia its first feeble experience with democracy and free parliamentary speech on current political issues.

Thus, with the beginning of the Turkish war, Panin began a lengthy downward course. He sought earnestly to terminate the conflict by 1772 or early 1773, but was blocked by the idiocies of the waning favorite, Grigory Orlov: had he been successful, he might have prevented or greatly mitigated the hardships of the Pugachev rebellion, which shook the foundations of the Russian Empire before Panin's brother Peter emerged from his informal Moscow exile to quell it. But then Orlov was succeeded by the all-powerful favorite Grigory Potemkin (later of Potemkin village fame), who persuaded Catherine to reorient her foreign policy toward Austria and expansionism, and away from Prussia and conservatism. With that, Panin's hand upon the tiller of Russian foreign policy weakened further, although he did not abandon his positions until 1781, and then not before, in 1780, he had formulated the policy of Russian "armed neutrality" which indirectly aided the struggle of the American colonies for their political independence.

Fonvizin, then, joined forces with Nikita Panin, with whose political outlook he agreed in almost every particular. At first he played a relatively modest role as a principal assistant to Panin, but later on, as the Panin party's actual power declined, he became one of its principal theoreticians and spokesmen.

By late 1769 Fonvizin was back in St. Petersburg, in the thick of policy affairs at the highest level and so busy that he scarcely had time to think, much less write anything lengthy or of much importance. Nearly everything having to do with Russia's foreign policy passed through Panin's hands, which meant that Fonvizin dealt with a steady stream of confidential documents. Many of them he transmitted to General Peter Panin, an eminent but testy military man who decided Catherine had slighted him after his successes early in the Turkish war and retired to Moscow, where he criticized her constantly, quite to her displeasure. Much of Panin's business during the early 1770s had to do with the abortive peace negotiations with Turkey; much else had to do with the details of the infamous partition of Poland among Russia, Prussia, and Austria in 1773. Fonvizin was involved in the haggling over the particulars of Poland's division among her enemies. For him this was merely a technical question suitable for negotiation among diplomats.

The early 1770s also saw many political intrigues directed against Panin and his supporters. In January of 1772 Fonvizin wrote to Peter Panin that all these things would sort themselves out. Most great men do not really receive their due while they are alive, he said, but he was sure that eventually the workings of history would distinguish "flattery and slander from truth itself" and the achievements of great men would be appreciated at their true value (II, 336). A bit later, referring to the peace negotiations with Turkey in another letter to Peter Panin, Fonvizin wrote:

All Europe, not to mention our Fatherland, knows *who is conducting our affairs and who is seeking peace.* In a word, no matter how the favor of the crowd may insult those who are truly worthy, the glory of the former will disappear along with the flatterers at the same time when that *favor itself vanishes;* but the glory of the latter will never die. (II, 395)

Another reason for the shakiness of Panin's position at the time—in addition to the difficulties of extracting Russia from an exhausting war—were the intrigues connected with the question of the succession to the throne. In the view of the Panin party, much hinged upon what would befall them when Paul reached his majority (eighteen years) in September of 1772. The group had placed its hopes in him. For a time in late 1771 it seemed they might be entirely dashed when Paul fell so critically ill as to be in danger of death. By November 21, however, Fonvizin was informing Peter Panin with relief that Paul was on the road to recovery (II, 364). He made a public, though anonymous, statement in a nicely printed brochure issued shortly thereafter and entitled *Slovo na vyzdorovlenie . . . Pavla Petrovicha* (Discourse on the Recovery of Paul Petrovich), in which he rendered thanks on behalf of the entire Russian nation for Paul's delivery from the perils of death.

Though this crisis passed, there remained the problem of whether Catherine would in fact yield the throne to her son once he came of age. Catherine was much too ambitious to do any such thing. Instead, she transformed what should have been a celebration of his majority into a celebration of his marriage, in the course of which the question of the succession was simply disregarded. For this purpose she contrived to postpone the entire ceremony for a year, to September of 1773, when Paul married Princess Wilhelmina of Hesse-Darmstadt. Fonvizin had no objection to the marriage: he appears to have found the Grand Duchess a paragon of virtue. "The goodness of her soul is written on her countenance," he wrote to a friend that September (II, 409). Three years later she would die in childbirth.

For reasons that are unclear and were probably unfounded, Catherine feared some sort of political initiative from the Panin party at this time, and took steps to neutralize it. However, far from undertaking any aggressive actions, the Panin group seems to have waited rather passively for some blow to descend upon it. In a long letter to his sister, probably written during the late summer of 1773, Fonvizin comments that everything has been prepared to separate Panin from the source of his power: his access to the Grand Duke. The members of the Panin group were being ousted from their places of residence, and only in September would it become clear how much of a foothold they might retain. His chief hope, he said, was to remain an "honest man" through all of this; his only wish was to be delivered from this "hell" of political intrigue with his honor intact (II, 355–56).

In the end the blow did fall, in the sense that Panin lost his position as tutor to Grand Duke Paul. But Catherine cushioned it very substantially. On September 22 she granted him a whole list of preferences and honors: he was made a field marshal and chief of the Foreign Service, given 9,000 serfs, 100,000 rubles for a home, a yearly pension of 30,000 rubles and a yearly salary of 14,000 rubles, a dining service worth 50,000 rubles, and several other very lucrative rewards. [10] In his turn Panin was also generous: he gave to his three chief assistants nearly half the serfs which he had received. Fonvizin's share of the Empress's largesse amounted to 1,180 serfs on an estate in Belorussia, a major source of income for him thereafter.

Despite all the political uncertainties of the early 1770s, Fonvizin used that time to good personal effect, for in 1774 he married Ekaterina Ivanovna Khlopova (1746–96). Born Rogikova, Ekaterina Ivanovna had eloped with her first husband, a man named Khlopov whose family were neighbors of the Fonvizins in Moscow. The elopement led to difficulties with her property, and Fonvizin evidently met her when he had to deal with a lawsuit over the matter. Fonvizin's biographer Petr Vyazemsky cites some evidence that she was Fonvizin's mistress for a time before their marriage, [11] and her first husband's fate is not very clear, but the two were properly married and seem to have had a reasonably happy life together, although it was not without its shoals. The couple moved into a pleasant house on Galerny Street in St. Petersburg, which, it is reported, was very artistically, tastefully, and comfortably furnished.

The Fonvizins did enjoy the good life. Most pictures of Fonvizin show him as fairly stout, which indicates that he enjoyed the pleasures of the table (he described them often enough in his correspondence). Vyazemsky mentions the fact that he loved to dress well. [12] Portraits also show him wearing the sort of wig fashionable at the time, though for him this was not so much a matter of fashion as of necessity, for he had very little hair. In December of 1771, when he was twenty-six, he wrote jokingly to a friend that a certain report would have caused his hair to stand on end if he had had any left (II, 395). Furthermore, he seems to have had rather poor vision (II, 431).

Fonvizin had more major afflictions, though. The most important was a tendency toward excruciating headaches, which he apparently inherited from his mother. In 1772 he wrote to Peter Panin that a headache the day before had left his thinking entirely confused (II, 388). Sometimes these attacks were caused by one of his intemperate rages; at least once, in 1769, he told Elagin that writing verse was causing his head to ache so that his physician had advised him to give it up (II, 401–402). Headaches plagued him all during his adult life, and may quite possibly have had some connection with the stroke he suffered in 1785.

Ekaterina Ivanovna had some difficulties with her health, too, which supplied the mundane motivation for Fonvizin's second trip abroad, in 1777–78, to Montpellier. Located in the South of France, at that time Montpellier was a renowned medical center, a rival to Paris. And it lived up to its reputation.

The Fonvizins set out upon their journey in September 1777, passing through Warsaw, Dresden, Leipzig, and a host of miniature German principalities. Entering France at Landau, they made their way through Strasbourg and Lyons to Montpellier. In most of the major cities they visited they were welcomed by Russian diplomatic representatives as a consequence of Fonvizin's standing in the Foreign Office. In foreign lands they devoted much effort to observing the customs of the local population. They were intelligent travelers who knew the languages of the nations they visited. They did not transport their own small corner of Russia with them.

Once Ekaterina Ivanovna's condition had been corrected, the Fonvizins traveled to Paris, arriving by March of 1778 and remaining until August of that year. By September they were on the move once more, and had returned to Russia by November. All during his travels Fonvizin recorded his fresh impressions in letters, primarily addressed to his family, but including a number to Peter Panin.

At home, the slow sapping of the Panin party's influence continued unabated until capped by Nikita Panin's resignation from his posts and retirement to his estate in 1781. The circumstances were such that Fonvizin could not long remain in government service thereafter, and on March 7, 1782, he petitioned the Empress for retirement, giving as his reason the "severe headaches from which I have suffered since my childhood."[13] His petition was granted on March 10, and Fonvizin became a private citizen, free to return to the pursuit of literature.

To be sure, Fonvizin had not deserted literature for politics altogether during the 1770s, but literary interests had greatly receded in his mind. After his original work *The Brigadier* of 1769, when he once more returned to the literary arena he again busied himself with translations. Thus in 1777 he published a rendering of a work by Antoine Thomas under the title *Pokhval'noe slovo Marku Avreliiu* (Eulogy of Marcus Aurelius), a tract in political philosophy dealing with the question of how a ruler ought to rule. A similar topic was at the heart of another translation, published anonymously in 1779 in the leading St. Petersburg newspaper. Entitled *Ta-Gio* (Or the Great Science, Containing within Itself the Highest Chinese Philosophy), the work is a compendium of Confucian teachings on the philosophy of rule.

These translations were a prelude to Fonvizin's theatrical masterpiece, the work through which his name has lived in Russian literature, *Nedorosl'* (The Minor, completed and premiered in 1782). Thus the year 1782 witnessed the end of Fonvizin's political career, while at the same time marking the zenith of his literary renown. The historian of the Panin party, David Ransel, has interpreted *The Minor* as a summary statement of that party's philosophical position. If it was, it also signaled the Panin party's withdrawal from the battlefield of politics as such to that of culture and literature.

IV   *Return to Moscow: Literature and Politics, 1782–92*

Following his resignation from government service, Fonvizin left St. Petersburg, that center of political intrigue, for his native Moscow, a more easygoing city. We do not know for certain when he again took up residence in his family home, but it must have been by the end of 1783 at the latest. He would reside principally in Moscow for what remained of his life.

The concluding months of 1782 and most of 1783 were a very busy and productive—though not entirely cheerful—time for Fonvizin. He had to expend some energy upon the staging of *The Minor*, for local officials were sometimes reluctant to stage a work critical of many aspects of contemporary society. Though successful in this, he was distressed when his friend and patron of so many years, Nikita Panin, died on March 13, 1783. Fonvizin, realizing that he was unusually qualified to assure Panin that place in history which he believed he deserved, published (anonymously) a brief and eulogistic biography of him entitled *Zhizn' grafa N. I. Panina* (Life of Count N. I. Panin). The work first came out in London in 1784, in French, and did not appear in a Russian translation for another two years. The biography, in addition to providing information on Panin's family background, his personal character, and his principles of statecraft, emphasized particularly his achievements in the area of foreign policy. Fonvizin also underlined the considerable impact which Panin had had—or so he believed—on the formation of the Grand Duke's outlook and character: the work ends with a letter from Paul to the archbishop of Moscow, in which the Grand Duke paid tribute to his teacher.

In the period after Panin's resignation and before his death, the Panin group had set about formulating a theoretical program for the conduct of affairs in a well-ordered state. The chief documents issuing from this effort were a draft statement of "fundamental rights" of the citizenry, composed chiefly by Peter Panin; and *"Rassuzhdenie o nepremennykh gosudarstvennykh zakonakh"* (A Discourse on Permanent Laws of the State) by Fonvizin, which, however, was not published during the author's lifetime: evidently Nikita Panin's untimely death discouraged further work on these programs. Fonvizin's *Discourse* is another general work of political philosophy on the proper relationship between ruler and ruled.

Fonvizin also sought to propagate other political ideas of his through translations and original writing. The chief such translation was the *Rassuzhdenie o natsional'nom liubochestii* (An Essay on National Patriotism, 1785), from an original by the German Johann Zimmermann dating from 1758. This *Essay* is a treatise on patriotism as the highest ideal of the citizen, the ideal for which he would sacrifice all. To be sure, the work does comment fairly extensively on the perils of chauvinism, but concludes that at that time a lack of patriotism was a greater danger than any excess of it.

The relationship between the man of temporal power and the man of moral authority at the highest level is discussed in a more original work, "Kallisfen" (Callisthenes), first published in a journal in 1786. Set at a safe distance in time and space—the Greece of Alexander the Great—the story describes the attempt of the philosopher Callisthenes, Aristotle's disciple, to influence Alexander the Great for the good. "Callisthenes" plainly has to do with the contest which Nikita Panin had waged for the mind of Catherine over against her various favorites.

Fonvizin did not limit his political critique of Catherine to translations and works of fiction set in ancient times. He was even prepared to carry the battle directly to her, at least in 1783. For in that year Catherine decided to encourage journalistic debate on political and cultural matters through the establishment of the periodical *Sobesednik liubitelei rossiiskogo slova* (Colloquy of Lovers of the Russian Word), edited by her close ally Princess Ekaterina Dashkova. To some extent her project succeeded all too well, especially when Fonvizin anonymously submitted to the journal his "Neskol'ko voprosov, mogushchikh vozbudit' v umnykh i chestnykh liudiakh osoblivoe vnimanie" (A Few Questions Which May Arouse Especial Interest in the Minds of Intelligent and Honest People). These rather sharply phrased "Questions" emphasized the author's contention that honest and straightforward people could not obtain advancement in the Russia of 1783. Catherine herself undertook to answer the questions, and her replies were often as testy as the queries had been. Fonvizin took the matter further in a letter in which he commented on some of the questions and answers. Evidently Catherine did not appreciate the entire exchange, and so brought it to a conclusion. The *Sobesednik* itself was terminated in September of 1784.

This acrimonious exchange of opinion—perhaps because it was cloaked in anonymity on both sides—did not lead to any sanctions against Fonvizin. In fact, when in the fall of 1783—again under the leadership of Princess Dashkova—the Russian Academy, modeled on the French Academy, came into existence, Fonvizin was there as a founding member, along with nearly all the other literary men of any consequence. Among its first tasks, the Academy undertook the compilation of a multi-volume dictionary of the Russian literary language. Fonvizin apparently had given some thought to this subject before, for at the Academy's session of November 11, 1783, he presented a "Nachertanie" (Outline) for the dictionary which was largely adopted for the Academy Dictionary which appeared from 1789 to 1794. Poor health, other commitments, and his move to Moscow prevented Fonvizin from participating actively in the work of compilation beyond its initial stages, but to him must go much of the credit for formulating the organizational concepts behind the first extensive dictionary of the Russian literary language.

Among Fonvizin's other commitments was a foreign journey of 1784 and 1785. By July of 1784 he and his wife had reached Riga, from which city they continued through Königsberg to Leipzig. In August and September they paid leisurely visits to such cities as Nürnberg, Augsburg, and Bozen (present-day Bolzano), with Fonvizin writing the same entertaining and perceptive sorts of letters to his family about his German observations as those he had composed during his visit to France some six years before. From Austria the couple made their way to Italy, reaching Florence by October 5. By early December the travelers had arrived, via Pisa, in Rome, where they remained until late April or early May of 1785. In early May they began the long trek home, stopping in Milan, Venice, Vienna, and Baden before returning to Moscow in the late summer.

The trip to Germany, Italy, and Austria was the last one the Fonvizins would venture primarily as tourists. For in Rome on this occasion Fonvizin suffered what must have been a preliminary attack which debilitated him physically and caused him to turn aside to the baths at Baden for relief. This apparently proved insufficient, for shortly after his return to Moscow, on August 29, 1785, he suffered a paralytic stroke which affected his speech, in addition to his arm and his leg. He would never fully recover from this illness, and it powerfully affected his mode and view of life during his last years. Henceforth he would spend much of his time, effort, and substance in traveling abroad for baths, trusting pathetically in one doctor after another, each of whom assured him that *he* could restore him to health. He did partially recover his speech and the use of his limbs, at least sufficiently to travel under the difficult conditions of those times, but his situation was constantly with him. In his correspondence for 1787 and 1789, for instance, he marked August 29 as the melancholy anniversary of his misfortune.

The Fonvizins' next journey, undertaken for reasons of health, lasted from June of 1786 through August 1787, and was spent primarily in Austria-Hungary for the sake of the baths. The psychological impact of his illness emerged in his delight at leaving Moscow, which he had come to hate intensely (II, 563), and in his journal entry made upon crossing the Russian border: "I silently thanked God for delivering me from the land [Russia] where I had suffered so much both physically and spiritually" (II, 568). But with the passage of time Fonvizin was happy enough to return to Russia. He was a compulsive traveler, who always wanted to be somewhere other than where he was at the moment.

In the summer of 1789 Fonvizin made a final effort to travel for a cure, journeying to Riga, Baldone, and Mitau (present-day Jelgava) while keeping a brief but informative diary. By now his health had so deteriorated that he began to detect flickers of alarm on the faces of old friends when they first saw him. Mineral water baths seemed no longer enough, and he resorted to "animal baths," which entailed placing his paralyzed arm and/or leg inside the entrails of a freshly slaughtered pig or bull. Each new doctor gave his fresh assurances, but Fonvizin's journal for 1789 ends on the fourth anniversary of his stroke, and on a somber note: "All day today the memory of my misfortune has unsettled my soul. Dr. Herz and the Surgeon, V, let some blood from under my tongue" (II, 580). After that it was back to Moscow, with little hope for the future.

It would be incorrect to conclude that Fonvizin was reduced to virtual inactivity during the years after 1785. His mind remained relatively quick, and he wanted very much to contribute what he could to Russian culture and literature. In 1766, it will be recalled, he had published a translation urging the nobility to engage in commerce. Fonvizin truly believed that the nobility should buttress the economic health of the state in this way, and, while always conscious of his gentry status, had put that theory into practice himself. He had combined his commercial interests with artistic ones by trading in paintings and art objects. His chief associate in this enterprise was Hermann Klostermann (1756–1838), a native of Holland who had come to Russia as a young boy and later owned a bookstore in St. Petersburg. According to Klostermann's memoirs,[14] Fonvizin and Klostermann first met in Paris during Fonvizin's visit there in 1777. At the time Fonvizin was acting as Nikita Panin's agent in the purchase of art objects and paintings, and Klostermann in turn acted as Fonvizin's agent, in addition to becoming a close personal friend of his.

Klostermann also handled Fonvizin's business affairs on several important occasions. For instance, when the Fonvizins needed some substantial sums for their trip to Italy in 1784, Klostermann sold their collection of books and art objects for more than 50,000 rubles. Fonvizin had also leased the Belorussian estate Panin had given him to a certain Baron Medem, in order to obtain a regular income therefrom. But the peasants rebelled against Medem, so that he could collect no income from them and could remit nothing to the Fonvizins. As a result Klostermann had to negotiate a loan to enable the Fonvizins to return to Russia. On the way to Moscow through Belorussia Fonvizin had a confrontation with Medem which was so unpleasant that it appears to have contributed to his stroke.[15] The situation of Fonvizin's peasants was so deplorable that many of them came, in an utterly impoverished state, to St. Petersburg seeking work, a rather embarrassing situation for a champion of humane treatment of serfs. Fonvizin's debts continued to accumulate, and when he was in Austria for the baths in 1787 he again had to borrow money to return home (II, 561). Vyazemsky comments that Fonvizin was very generous with his money, of which he had little, but he did keep excellent accounts. "The thing is," Vyazemsky adds drily, "that it is easier to note down your expenses than it is to refrain from incurring them."[16]

His financial needs must have encouraged Fonvizin to seek some income from his pen, since by the 1780s Russian literature had developed to the point where a writer could at least obtain some supplementary income from his writing. He looked upon publication strictly as a commercial matter, and indeed he could scarcely afford to issue anything at a loss. Thus, when he publicly announced his intention to start a journal in 1788 entitled *Drug chestnykh liudei, ili Starodum* (The Friend of Honest Men, or Starodum—Starodum was the leading positive character of *The Minor*),[17] Fonvizin carefully stipulated the cost of the subscription and what each subscriber could anticipate for his money: he also deposited material intended for early issues for private inspection at Klostermann's bookshop. But he also declared that a minimum of 750 subscriptions would have to be in hand by March 1, 1788, for the project to proceed. We do not know whether the necessary number of readers entered their subscriptions, and even if they did, the police forbade the periodical's appearance.[18]

With the failure of this project, Fonvizin considered publishing his collected writings, many of which had originally appeared anonymously. On May 26, 1788, he printed an advertisement for such a collected edition—this time under his own name—in *Sankt-Peterburgskie vedomosti* (St. Petersburg News). The announcement listed a number of works which would be included in the five-volume set, for which a definite price was stipulated.[19] Quite possibly an insufficient number of subscribers were found here too, or else the police raised objections once more, for this collection never came out. The discovery of the announcement, though, has enabled us to attribute several anonymous works to him with certainty.

At the very end of his life, in 1791, Fonvizin once more thought of printing his collected works, but in the years of the French Revolution the likelihood of his receiving permission for such a thing was entirely remote.

His physical incapacity, financial distress, and inability to publish led Fonvizin to turn his thoughts to things eternal, and the consolation of religion. An event which made a profound impression upon Russian society at the conclusion of Fonvizin's life was the sudden death of Catherine's fabulously wealthy and powerful favorite, Grigory Potemkin. Death came for him as he traveled across the steppe, and the man who had ordered the fortunes of one of the greatest powers in Europe lay down on the grass by the side of the road and departed this life. The poet Gavriil Derzhavin paid impressive poetic tribute to this illustration of ultimate human powerlessness, and Fonvizin too wrote of it in a very short prose-work, "Rassuzhdenie o suetnoi zhizni chelovecheskoi" (Essay on the Vanity of Human Life, II, 79–80). After quoting extensively from the Scriptures, Fonvizin applies the lesson of Potemkin's death to his own life. He had been struck down by the Almighty, he said, just when he was returning from abroad puffed up with intellectual pride: "then the Allknowing One, seeing that my talents might be more harmful than helpful, deprived me of the ability to express myself by the written and spoken word" (II, 80). It is said also that Fonvizin once visited the chapel of Moscow University and presented himself to the students as an example of one "punished for his free-thinking."[20]

The principal literary fruit of Fonvizin's religious penitence was his fragmentary autobiography, *Chistoserdechnoe priznanie v delakh moikh i pomyshleniiakh* (An Open-Hearted Confession of My Deeds and Thoughts), written evidently in the final year or two of his life, which breaks off at the end of the 1760s. Although he explicitly mentions Rousseau's *Confessions* as a model for it, in its religious orientation Fonvizin's autobiography is more reminiscent of St. Augustine's *Confessions*. Each subdivision of the work in its present form is preceded by a religious formulation; the work as a whole was designed to serve as an intellectual expiation for what the author regarded as the sins of his youth, especially his religious doubts.

At the same time, Fonvizin's confession provides much interesting information on his personality which we could not obtain from any other source. At least in the back of his mind he must have known that his autobiography would to a large degree determine the manner in which posterity would view him. He would now repeat for himself the historical service which he had once rendered to Nikita Panin.

The heavily religious coloration of the *Confession* does demand some explanation. Soviet scholars are given to dismissing this aspect of the confession as the aberration of a sick man nearing death, and to arguing that religion normally meant little in his life. As proof of this they point to the very passages in the *Confession* where Fonvizin describes his atheistic and blasphemous St. Petersburg circle. Other evidence, however, indicates that all through his life Fonvizin was a serious and intelligent adherent of Russian Orthodoxy. In the *Confession* itself he characterizes his parents' home and his upbring-ing as deeply religious, and speaks of both of his parents as "pious" (II, 87). Later on, when he left home and found himself in an antireligious ambience, even then he wrote to his sister that he was observing all the rites of Holy Week, although, to be sure, he was youthfully flip in his phraseology.[21]

In his more mature years, and especially during his journeys abroad of 1777–78 and 1784–85, Fonvizin took a lively interest in the religious and liturgical customs of Western Europe, constantly comparing them to Orthodox theology and liturgy. For instance, upon attending an All Souls Day requiem in Strasbourg in 1777, he found the garb and actions of the priests so strange that he almost burst into laughter: "It was just a comedy," he said (II, 418). A short time later, in Montpellier, he described a religious ceremony in great detail, and again found the Catholic ritual so strange as to be humorous (II, 425–27). This journey to France, however, was his first extended visit abroad, and since probably he was seeing these ceremonies for the first time, he simply tended to reject that which was unfamiliar to him.

By 1784–85, during his sojourn in Italy, Fonvizin adopted a more sober view of the Catholic Church. He detested many things about Italy, but he found St. Peter's breathtakingly impressive—"It seems as if God had created this temple just for Himself" (II, 531)—and visited it twice daily when he could. During Holy Week of 1785 he followed the services in Rome very closely. In general he preferred the Orthodox to the Catholic liturgy, believing that Western ceremony was too "theatrical" and had "too little to do with direct piety" (II, 543). But he was intensely interested in the symbolism of Western ceremonial, and discussed it as one who had thought extensively about it (see II, 556). And he was deeply moved when he heard the impressive music of what was probably the liturgy for Tenebrae in Holy Week in the Sistine Chapel. "I don't know of anything in the world," he wrote to Peter Panin, "which might touch the soul so deeply as this singing. The music is so simple that when you see it written down you simply cannot comprehend the source of its indescribable beauty" (II, 555).

In short, Fonvizin's travel letters give ample contemporary evidence of his intelligent interest in religious questions well before his paralytic attack. After 1785 he probably became a bit more cantankerously "Russian" in his religion. On the way to Austria in 1786 he and his wife stopped in Kiev to make the rounds of the churches, monasteries, and crypts in that "New Jerusalem" of ancient Russia (II, 567). There is more than a touch of anti-Semitism in his comments on Poland (II, 568). And the God of his last writings is an Old Testament God, a God who punishes for offenses and sends plagues upon those who love Him. If, at the end, the quality of Fonvizin's religion was altered somewhat, the interest in religion itself had always been present, from his earliest youth.

Despite his parlous health, Fonvizin's love for the theater did not desert him, and one of his last artistic works was still another play, *Vybor guvernera* (The Selection of a Tutor), a brief and obviously unfinished comedy about a pretentious noble couple seeking a tutor for their son, who are so emptyheaded as to prefer a superficial Frenchman over a serious and honest Russian. Apparently it was this play which the writer brought with him on his last evening in society, November 30, 1792. The place was the St. Petersburg home of the poet and statesman Gavriil Derzhavin, the chronicler was a budding poet of the Sentimentalist school, Ivan Dmitriev.[22] Fonvizin arrived about six, Dmitriev recalled, assisted by two young officers. One of Fonvizin's companions read the play aloud while the author indicated his approval with his eyes and motions of the head, since he could speak only with difficulty. Fonvizin took an encouraging interest in Dmitriev, querying him about his reading, especially his reading of Fonvizin's works. In spite of everything, Fonvizin retained the capacity to entertain his audiences, Dmitriev reports. Fonvizin took his leave of them at about eleven that evening. The next day, December 1, he was no more.

Fonvizin was buried in St. Petersburg, in the Lazarev cemetery (now the older section) of the cemetery of the Alexander Nevsky monastery. He was laid to rest near Lomonosov. The inhabitants of the capital did little to preserve his memory, for a century later, in 1891, a major St. Petersburg newspaper reported that his grave was neglected and difficult to find, being located in a depression which collected snow, rain, and mud.[23] But if St. Petersburg was disgracefully inattentive, the common people of Moscow remembered him. In the middle of the nineteenth century an investigator reported that the Fonvizin home had in its time been known all over the city. Though it had long since been razed, the lane on which it had once stood was called Denis Lane by the people, and the public baths which occupied its site were known as the Denis baths.[24]

CHAPTER 2

Beginnings of a Literary Career

I   The Decade of the 1760s: Intellectual Currents

FONVIZIN's publishing career began in the brief span between 1760 and the beginning of Catherine's reign, and in many ways illustrates characteristic interests and attitudes of that important decade.

There exist certain striking parallels between the Russia of the 1760s and that of the 1860s, in the sense that the dominant intellectual influence in both decades was a rationalistic skepticism leading to a questioning of the established order. In the 1760s all received traditions and all political institutions ideally were subjected to the test of reason, and rejected if they were found lacking. The French culture of Voltaire's time was the primary source of this skepticism in Russia, a skepticism which frequently expressed itself as outright atheism, or at least agnosticism concerning the origins of the universe or the proper source of temporal authority. This skepticism also occasioned a generation gap, as the younger generation rejected the beliefs and allegiances of the older generation. In all these respects, the generation of the 1760s was a harbinger of the much more powerful and influential generation of the 1860s in Russia.

Fonvizin admired Voltaire's writings—as did Catherine herself—and translated some of them into Russian. His own mind had a naturally skeptical bent quite congruent with the Voltairean approach. Though he overstated the case, one student of Fonvizin has written that his early works were "imbued with a spirit of corrosive skepticism which spared nothing and stopped at nothing."[1] The formulation is largely true, and indeed Fonvizin even applied his skepticism to Voltaire himself. Once, in the Paris of 1778, he saw the "famous man" himself at the theater. Later Fonvizin attended a meeting of the Academy of Sciences at which Voltaire was also present, being rather elderly and spare at the time. "I was sitting very close to him," he wrote, "and didn't take my eyes off his relics [*moshchi*]" (II, 449). Fonvizin's choice of the word "relics," ordinarily used of saints, demonstrates how humorously skeptical he could be even about such a revered intellectual.

In his autobiography Fonvizin recalls a time during the 1760s when he fell in with a circle of atheists. If he did not share their atheism, he at least allowed his native skepticism free rein while among them. The principal literary fruit of this period is the short poem "Epistle to My Servants," first published in 1769.[2] Here the narrator, who may be equated with Fonvizin, addresses to each of his three servants the philosophical query: why was the universe created, and what is the purpose of our existence? The three servants answer variously. The first, Mikhail Shumilov, replies that he was born to serve, and that it is not his place to puzzle over such questions. The second servant, the coachman Vanka, though he begins by saying that he is not even literate, has yet concluded that there is no reason at all to the universe: "Everything in the world is vanity, it seems to me" (II, 210). There is no such thing as truth or justice; all are concerned only with money, including the clergy, who would deceive the Almighty himself it it would profit them financially. So Vanka also concludes that no one comprehends the aim of our existence. The narrator finally turns to his servant Petrushka, who, in a variant on the Deistic hypothesis of the clockwork universe, claims that God has merely wound human beings up like dolls and set them bobbing about on a table. Petrushka also believes that nobody knows the answer to the question. All three servants then present the query to their master, who replies that he is entirely as ignorant as they on the matter.

The "Epistle to My Servants," though explicitly agnostic, incorporates certain metaphysical assumptions tending toward the conclusion that Creation is based upon evil and social injustice. Though these assumptions logically exclude the possibility that the universe might have been designed for good, neither do they inevitably reach the conclusion that the universe may deliberately have been designed to reward evil. This intertwining of theological reasoning with philosophical skepticism results in agnosticism in the truest sense. Fonvizin is an idealist who believes Creation should be good, but realizes that it is not, and thus arrives at an openly agnostic (though not atheistic) stance. This division between idealism and skepticism would remain a constant of his approach, even though in most of his writing he expressed at least the implicit confidence that the good would ultimately prevail.

II   *The Decade of the 1760s: Political Aspects*

Fonvizin's political idealism expressed itself most clearly in his translations of several treatises published during the 1760s. The most interesting of these are the version of Coyer's *La Noblesse commercante* published in 1766, and a more original compilation of article length which he worked over in 1764–66 but which remained unpublished until 1959, "Sokrashchenie o vol'nosti frantsuzskogo dvorianstva" (Extract on the Freedom of the French Nobility).

The "Extract" is an attempt on Fonvizin's part to deal with the problem of political liberty in the Russian setting, at a time when restrictions upon the freedom of action and movement of the peasantry were being tightened. Fonvizin argues that the French nobility must always have enjoyed political liberty, especially since that nobility elected a king whenever the throne was vacant; he claims that it would be a logical contradiction for the French nobility not to have been free. From the nobility he passes to the Third Estate, calling it the "soul of society," and pointing out that this class has produced many great men and that any nation with pretensions to Great Power status must encourage it. Fonvizin also contends that the lower classes should enjoy a modicum of liberty, although he treads very carefully when he applies to Russian society the conclusions following from his discussion of France's historical situation:

In short, Russia should possess: 1) a completely free nobility, 2) an entirely liberated third estate, and 3) a people engaged in agriculture, who, though not entirely free, at least should have the hope of becoming such. . . . (II, 116)

Still, since the economic status of the Russian gentry at the time depended upon serfdom, and the power of the state depended upon the economic health of the nobility, Fonvizin evidently found it expedient not to press the question of freedom for the lower classes by publishing his article.

On the other hand, Fonvizin also felt that the nobility should not rely wholly upon agriculture, and serf labor, for its support. The Russian nobility traditionally held that it was improper for noblemen to engage in commerce. Instead, they should dedicate their energies to managing their estates. Since they had ultimately received those estates from the Crown, they in turn owed the Crown service, either in the military or the civil bureaucracy, without any particular further compensation. The history of the relationship between the Crown and the Russian nobility in the eighteenth century revolves largely around the latter's attempts to strengthen their legal authority over their serfs while simultaneously eliminating their legal obligations to the state.

Fonvizin did not share the attitude of his class toward commerce, which was why he chose to translate the *Commercial Nobility,* a work which had defended his point of view in a political debate in France some ten years earlier. The heart of Coyer's argument is to be found in the sentences: "Commerce is the soul of the state" (II, 168), and "Commerce elevates the nobility" (II, 171). Coyer-Fonvizin held that Russia's Peter the Great had understood the advantages of a commercial nobility, and England and Holland had provided excellent examples of world power attained through commerce. Military power depends upon economic strength, and therefore great ages in history have occurred when commerce flourished. The nobility itself, the argument went, would derive benefits from commerce, including simple physical exercise and the rewards of an occupation, to avert the plague of idleness which beset the upper classes. In short, Coyer and Fonvizin maintained that there was nothing at all demeaning in commercial enterprises. If the gentry enter business, they will not only strengthen the state, but will also buttress the economic foundations of their own class. Had the nobility taken Fonvizin's advice, it might have weathered its economic difficulties much more comfortably when the serfs were liberated nearly a century later.

At least Fonvizin followed his own commercial prescriptions, although he could not induce many of his fellow gentry to follow his example. But he did what lay within his power in the 1760s to advance the position that the nobility should be both politically free and economically useful to the state.[3]

III   *The Decade of the 1760s: Literary and Cultural Aspects*

By 1760 modern Russian literature was still very much in its infancy, having only begun to cast off its ecclesiastical matrix following the death of Peter the Great in 1725. Most of the important figures of Russian literature between 1730 and 1760—Antiokh Kantemir, Vasily Trediakovsky, Mikhail Lomonosov, Alexander

Sumarokov—had worked in the poetic genres, especially the ode and the verse satire. There simply was no appreciable prose tradition in existence when Fonvizin appeared upon the scene. Moreover, several great figures of early eighteenth-century literature lived into the 1760s and could defend the tenets of Neoclassical and Baroque literature through which they had made their reputations. The 1760s would witness clashes of several conflicting currents, none of which would gain a clear-cut victory over its particular rival. Fonvizin combines in one person some of these crosscurrents in an instructive way.

One such conflict was that between the poetic genres and the prose genres. Russian Neoclassicism was generally associated with the predominance of verse genres, and thus it is not surprising to find the young Fonvizin experimenting with the writing of odes and encouraging his sister to produce verse as well. In the 1760s he wrote several pieces in quite acceptable verse, and sometimes even very good verse; although later he wrote primarily in prose, even in the 1780s he occasionally resorted to verse. In this he reflects the tendency of Russian literature as a whole between 1760 and 1790, a period in which the poetic genres lost their previous dominance, but were not driven from the scene, and indeed existed in a state of approximate equilibrium with prose genres.

One of Fonvizin's earliest attempts at verse was his translation of Voltaire's *Alzire*, dating from 1762. The ambition of his experiment becomes clear if we recall that he was only seventeen at the time and had been studying French for only some two years, in addition to being a novice at writing in Russian. Subsequently the poem—in which Voltaire called upon Christians to behave humanely in exporting their culture to other lands, and argued that primitives might even be superior to civilized people—was on several occasions cited as a horrible example of incompetent translation.[4] One particularly egregious mistranslation, in which Fonvizin confused the French words *sabre* and *sable* to come up with a line speaking of "powerless marbles transformed into sand," has been repeatedly quoted to discredit Fonvizin's abilities as a translator. But Alexis Strycek, after comparing the original with the translation more carefully, arrives at a more positive evaluation of the accuracy of the translation—if not the quality of Fonvizin's verse—than many of his earlier critics.[5]

In fact, a scant two years later, his command of French by now much improved, Fonvizin essayed another verse translation from the French in the play *Korion*, a considerable achievement for a young man still short of twenty. It describes the tribulations of a nobleman who had abandoned Moscow for the country after betraying his beloved and seeks to end his life by suicide, in solitude. After he takes poison, believing the end is near, he is suddenly reunited with his beloved and realizes that he could regain happiness with her if only he had not already set his irrevocable course toward death. At this point his servant informs him that he had substituted water for the poison, and that his master is in no danger. The characters then presumably live happily ever after.

In addition to the fact that it was translated in verse, *Korion* represents another important element in the literary milieu of the 1760s as a "Russified" work.

In its formative stages a literature understandably relies heavily upon translations from more advanced literatures. In Pushkin's "Queen of Spades" the old Countess, a relic of the eighteenth century, always asks for French novels, and cannot believe that there is any such thing as a Russian novel. If she was raised in the early 1760s, there was considerable justification for her opinion. Fonvizin, we know, began his literary career with direct translations, his first such book being Holberg's *Fables*. [6] An even more ambitious attempt was his translation of the four volumes of *Séthos*. Apparently Fonvizin first worked from a German version, then shifted to the original as his command of French improved. He was absorbed in his work over this tale of "heroic virtue," and mentioned it several times in his personal correspondence of the 1760s. Still another translation of an appropriately moral sort was the brief "Torg semi muz" (Bargaining of the Seven Muses), published in Reichel's *Sobranie luchshikh sochinenii* in 1762. This tale describes the results of Jupiter's sending the Muses to earth to offer certain goods for sale: intellect, virtue, health, long life, intellectual pleasures, honor, a box filled with gold (I, 412–16). Each Muse arouses varying responses in offering her good for sale: the sellers of intellect and virtue, for instance, find no takers for their wares.

Fonvizin continued to publish direct translations through the 1760s. In general, translations never disappeared from the market, but toward the middle of the 1760s Russian authors felt the need to produce writings more national in coloration, and embraced the concept of Russianization, intermediate between translation and original writing. Russianization entailed minor changes in translating the original: its heroes would be given Russian names, the action would take place in Russia amid Russian place names; occasional

references to specifically Russian conditions or events might be
inserted so that the reader might delude himself that he was
confronted with a genuinely original Russian work. Vladimir Lukin
was a leading exponent of this approach in Russian dramaturgy of the
1760s; Elagin tried his hand at it, and so did Fonvizin in *Korion*. His
play was supposedly set near Moscow and featured a rather forward
and enterprising servant called Andrey. Still, the major characters,
who are of the nobility, bear such generalized Neoclassical names as
Korion and Menander, so that the play was by no means completely
Russified, for the Neoclassical tradition was still strong. Furthermore, Fonvizin shared Lukin's approach to Russification for only a
short time. As one scholar has put it, "Lukin did not understand that
the content of a comedy must be provided by the life of a particular
society."[7] Fonvizin did grasp this truth, as he would demonstrate
with his first great comedy, *The Brigadier*. In short, he quickly
moved beyond both direct and Russified translation, although he did
not abandon the former entirely.

A third important literary conflict of the 1760s in which Fonvizin
participated was that between a declining Neoclassicism and an
emergent Sentimentalism. Fonvizin evidently believed that the end
was nearing for the Neoclassical tragedy as represented in the works
of, say, Sumarokov: he felt that such writings were now fair game for
travesty. In a letter of December 1763 to his sister, he commented
irreverently on the tragedy, that classical Neoclassical form: "Myself
I'm burning with desire to compose a tragedy, so that by my hand
there will perish at least a half-dozen heroes, and if I really get angry
I won't leave a single living person in the theater" (II, 326). His play
Korion represented a travesty of the Neoclassical tragedy both in its
general plot and in its language. The latter may be illustrated by a
deliberately overblown passage from a speech of Korion's delivered
when he mistakenly thinks he is at the point of death:

I see eternal night! The doors of the grave stand open!
My limbs grow numb . . . my blood flows cold . . . the light goes dim . . .
My heart flutters . . . my spirit leaves my body . . .
I'm tortured, torn, trapped by anguish most horrible. . . .

(I, 41)

The literary current which sought to replace a declining Neoclassicism was that of Sentimentalism, particularly promoted by the
enigmatic literary adventurer Fedor Emin (ca. 1735–70), who re-

leased a flood of original and translated Sentimentalist novels onto the Russian market between 1763 and 1766. Sentimentalism tended to blunt the edges of human conflict by emphasizing the feelings, the awareness of the heart; it applauded the capacity of the sensitive man to shed tears. It downgraded the importance of the intellect and shifted attention from the great and universal questions of statecraft, honor, and duty—which had preoccupied Neoclassical writers—to problems of romantic love and the concrete individual. In the 1760s Sentimentalism made a strong bid for literary domination, but Neoclassicism did not yield without a struggle and continued to survive on a more or less equal basis with Sentimentalism through the 1770s. Eventually, however, in the 1780s Neoclassicism yielded its pride of place, and Sentimentalism prevailed in the literary arena.

Fonvizin's major contribution to the Sentimentalist current was his translation of *Joseph* (1769). A lengthy retelling of the story of Joseph and his brothers, the work begins with a partial invocation to Salomon Gessner, the Swiss writer and exponent of European Sentimentalism. *Joseph* then describes its hero's sale into slavery by his brothers, his prediction of the seven lean and seven fat years, his becoming a powerful official in Egypt, and finally his return to his father and his family. Conflict and tragedy are blunted: the author seeks primarily to evoke a mood of melancholy but enjoyable reflection in his reader. A central phrase in Sentimentalist literature is "pleasant melancholy," one which occurs in the description of Joseph's trip to view the sufferings of the Egyptian people during the famine in Canto Six: "Joseph, sailing near this shore [of the Nile], yields to his soul's inclination and gives himself over to pleasant melancholy" (I, 532). Again, Bitaube writes that "sensitive people" are bound by some mysterious ties to those places where "they have wept over their troubles" (I, 495). When Joseph languishes in slavery, he declines to join his fellow slaves in rebelling against their oppressors, preferring servitude to committing the sins of murder and violence (I, 499–50). In Sentimentalist literature things tend to work out in the end: the dead are not really dead, tragedies evaporate, and virtue prevails. Thus Joseph rejoins his family, forgives the brother most responsible for betraying him, and marries the woman who had remained faithful to him even though she had given him up for dead.

Joseph proved a popular translation: it appeared in a fourth edition in 1790, and Vyazemsky mentions its having appeared most recently in 1819.[8] The Sentimentalist poet Ivan Dmitriev (1760–1837) consid-

ered Fonvizin a forerunner of the Sentimentalist school in his
translation of *Joseph*.[9]

Still, Sentimentalism did not really fit Fonvizin's character and
left few traces in his later work. He was most fundamentally a satirist.
Satire requires sharp edges and quick humor, and cannot coexist with
hazy melancholy. Satire, which had flourished in the Classical and
Neoclassical tradition, almost ceased to exist during the ascendancy
of the Sentimentalist school.

To be sure, Fonvizin did not arrive at a correct assessment of his
own literary talent immediately. During the early 1760s his sister had
pressed him *not* to follow his satirical bent, and in a letter of
December 1762 he promised her that he would write no more satires
(II, 326). But 1762 had witnessed the first Russian publication of the
verse satires of Antiokh Kantemir (1708–44), an uncompromisingly
intellectual Neoclassical satirist with literary roots firmly fixed in the
tradition of Juvenal and Boileau. Kantemir's name never occurs in
Fonvizin's correspondence, but it is difficult to believe that Fonvizin
did not find in him a kindred soul.[10] Indirect proof of this is provided
by a fragment of a verse satire—almost certainly written in the 1760s
but not published in Fonvizin's lifetime—which in spirit is very
reminiscent of Kantemir, and whose title, "K umu moemu" (To My
Mind), recalls almost precisely the title of Kantemir's first satire. If
Fonvizin were to follow in Kantemir's footsteps, he must ineluctably
adopt a generally Neoclassical view of the world, and reject Sentimentalism.

By 1769 Fonvizin had overcome the sheer skepticism of the
"Epistle to My Servants" and realized that his talents lay in satire. For
the year 1769, which saw the appearance of the Sentimentalist
Joseph, also saw the composition of Fonvizin's first great original
satirical work, *The Brigadier*. Fonvizin abandoned Sentimentalism as
a literary approach, and adhered to the Neoclassical comedy tradition
as the matrix of his satire. In order to understand *The Brigadier*, we
must know something more of the Fonvizinian conception of satire.[11]

CHAPTER 3

The Brigadier

I Background of a Play

*T*he *Brigadier* was a genuine milestone in the development of the original Russian comedy. It also signaled the maturing of Fonvizin as a literary artist, indicating that the twenty-four-year-old author had discovered the genre which best suited him. Through that genre he would exercise lasting influence on the history of Russian literature.

The play's plot is constructed upon interlocking marital triangles involving two families. The first family is that of the Brigadier and the Brigadier's wife *(Brigadirsha),* whose son Ivanushka has been betrothed to Sofya, the daughter of the Counsellor *(Sovetnik)* and stepdaughter of the Counsellor's second wife *(Sovetnitsa).* As the play opens, these characters have gathered to make the final arrangements for the marriage at the bride's home, where all the action takes place.

Sofya has no desire at all to marry the blockhead Ivanushka, a caricature of the *petit maître* whose one wish is to transform himself into a Frenchman. Sofya's affections are pledged instead to Dobrolyubov, whose name signifies "lover of the good." In the end it is their marriage which is arranged, and not that of Sofya and Ivanushka.

The plot is complicated by the fact that each husband in the play—the Brigadier and the Counsellor—is smitten with passion for the other's wife, and makes unreciprocated advances to her. But the wives fail to respond, though for quite different reasons. The Brigadier's wife does not succumb to the Counsellor's blandishments because she believes in adhering to her marriage vows, but also because she is simply too dense to grasp what her suitor desires. The Counsellor's wife, on the other hand, is sufficiently worldly-wise to realize that the Brigadier is courting her, but she has in the meantime

49

become enamored of Ivanushka, since she too lives and breathes only for things French.

The plot, then, consists in the tangling and untangling of these roughly symmetrical love intrigues. All is eventually sorted out, husband remains with wife, and the way is clear for Sofya and Dobrolyubov to be joined in matrimony.

Our knowledge of the circumstances under which *The Brigadier* was written and first presented to the public is spotty. Some scholars have argued that Fonvizin began work on the comedy as early as 1766, but the general consensus of scholarly opinion now is that it was written at the very end of the decade, most probably in 1768 and 1769, while Fonvizin was residing with his family in Moscow.[1] In the contemporary documentation we first learn of it from a letter to Elagin, which Fonvizin's editor dates no more precisely than 1769 (II, 401–402). At the time the letter was sent the play was evidently complete, for Fonvizin spoke of bringing it with him should he be required to return to St. Petersburg immediately. He was understandably nervous over his first substantial original literary effort, and hoped that his superior and literary senior would serve as a prepublication critic. Shortly before, he said, he had read a satire directed against the author of some witless comedy, and Fonvizin, satirist though he was himself, did not care to be subjected to the same treatment. Fonvizin commented that he was not among those with such an exaggerated idea of their literary talent as to account themselves a Russian Molière, or even a Russian Destouches (II, 402). He surely hoped that Elagin, the head of the state theaters, would assist him in staging the work. So far as we know, however, Elagin was entirely uncooperative: he apparently gave Fonvizin no counsel in advance of publication and did not help him with the play's staging. Indeed, it is not even known when the play received its premiere performance.

As things turned out, the high officials who promoted the play were not those with literary pretensions, like Elagin, but rather men without them—Catherine's favorite, Grigory Orlov, and Nikita Panin. Upon returning to St. Petersburg, presumably in the early summer of 1769, Fonvizin gave readings of the play, quite successfully, as he thought. When word of the new comedy reached Orlov's ears, the favorite asked him to bring it along if he were going to be in Peterhof, the royal residence near St. Petersburg, in late June or early July. Fonvizin of course did so, and soon had the opportunity to read the play to the Empress herself. Catherine complimented him on his work, and he departed quite pleased (II, 97).

After this reading and others, his play became the talk of the Court at Peterhof. That led in turn to his first close contact with Nikita Panin, when the latter asked him to give a reading for the Grand Duke Paul and his associates, which he did a few days later in St. Petersburg. He recalled in his autobiography that he realized the first objective of his play had been achieved when his hearers burst into "uproarious laughter" a few moments after he began; and his more serious objective was reached afterwards, when Panin praised his work glowingly, characterizing it in a sentence which has remained attached to it ever since: "This is the first comedy ever written about our social mores" (II, 97–99). Panin then invited Fonvizin to give a reading at his own home, and he entered the literary and intellectual circle surrounding the Grand Duke. For Fonvizin, the path to political advancement lay through literature.

Thereafter Fonvizin was asked to read his comedy in one aristocratic salon after another, and his play became the talk of the capital (II, 99–100). He could hardly have hoped that *The Brigadier* would produce a more striking impact upon high society than it did in fact. Even more important, the play immediately became a minor classic, as the Soviet scholar Dmitry Blagoy points out: characters from the play cropped up in the satirical journals of immediately succeeding years, and quotations from it entered the living language in the form of sayings and proverbs.[2] No beginning author could have asked for a more lasting and resounding success.

II *Satire and the Neoclassical Comedy*

To be sure, some nineteenth-century critics found it difficult to accept *The Brigadier* as a legitimate work of art. Something was missing, they felt, something to do with the relationship between satire and comedy. The leading Russian critic of the nineteenth century, Vissarion Belinsky, was among these: he drew the issue very sharply when he wrote that both *The Brigadier* and *The Minor* were "the fruit of an attempt by Russian satire to become comedy."[3] Writing at almost the same time, a less prominent critic, Stepan Dudyshkin, made the same point in the course of a lengthy review of a new edition of Fonvizin's works: "And so *The Brigadier* is not a comedy either in its action or in its characters; it is something closer to a satire on society, and therefore not an artistic work."[4] A proper understanding of the play, then, requires that we examine its position at the intersection of the satirical tradition in Russian literature, on the one hand, with the tradition of the Neoclassical comedy on the other.

Nearly all historians of Russian literature would agree that Fonvizin was the outstanding satirist of his day, and would link his name with Kantemir's as the two leading eighteenth-century Russian satirists. This does not mean that there were not noticeable satirical elements in the work of many lesser writers, as well as in the writing of such prominent figures with roots in the Neoclassical tradition as Lomonosov, Derzhavin, and especially Sumarokov. The satirical tradition was very strong in the Russia of the eighteenth century, and the targets of the satirists' scorn remained remarkably constant throughout that period. They included: the ignorance of the ordinary man and the official alike, and their unwillingness to enlighten themselves; greed, and the grasping for preferment; the problem of true nobility as deriving from the nobility of the individual soul or the prominence of one's ancestors; relationships between the sexes, especially within marriage; injustice and corruption at the middle and lower levels of the bureaucracy; and, in the latter half of the century, Gallomania, the fashionable craze for everything French. These and related questions attracted the creators of the Russian satirical tradition who derided phenomena of actual reality in the name of a higher ideal.

There were always those who cast doubt upon the utility of satirical writing. One such was Mikhail Kheraskov, who in 1760 wrote a programmatic poem, "K satiricheskoi muze" (To the Muse of Satire), arguing that there was no point in attempting to eliminate social evils through satirical works since no one would admit that there were any shortcomings in contemporary society, and therefore people were not susceptible to reform. Could a writer hope to eliminate, say, drunkenness by his pen, he asked? Of course not. "We have no faults," he concluded sarcastically, and it was unrealistic to assume that any substantial social improvements could be effected through literature.[5] For a time even Fonvizin seems to have entertained the argument that satire accomplishes no good purpose: the burden of his fragment "To My Mind" is precisely that the task of reforming "fools" in society is beyond the capacity of any writer, for a "fool will remain a fool forever." Moreover, by what authority does the satirical writer arrogate to himself the right to preach to others (I, 216)? But a born satirist like Fonvizin could not indefinitely deny his own nature. At the inception of the satirical journals of 1769, two leading figures in that movement—Nikolay Novikov and Catherine herself—debated the nature of satire. At least in theory, Novikov defended the idea of satire directed against particular individuals recognizable to the reading audience, whereas Catherine held that satire should be general, directed against common vices, on the grounds that most faults were really the result of moral weakness rather than conscious evil intent. From the strictly literary point of view, Catherine was correct. Novikov was too much of a journalist, one who wanted to "expose" current abuses. Works attacking particular individuals rarely retain any interest for general readers a century later, since they lack any direct knowledge of the persons attacked. One of the accusations brought against Sumarokov's comedies was that he used them to even scores with his literary and intellectual rivals.[6] Although he made no explicit statements on this subject, Fonvizin adhered to Catherine's view of satire, for it is impossible to identify any well-known prototypes for his leading comic characters, although some have attempted to do so. To be sure, in his autobiography he mentions having used the dim-witted mother of the Moscow girl whom he briefly courted as the model for the Brigadier's wife (II, 89), but he clearly regarded her as an instance of a general type, and not anyone whom a theater audience would know. He no doubt would have been distressed if she had recognized herself in his fictional creation.

It is helpful to distinguish between the uses of humor and the uses of satire in the comedy. The humorist writes purely for the sake of entertainment, whereas the satirist seeks to correct social *mores* through the power of laughter. We may surmise that the distinguished men who heard Fonvizin read *The Brigadier* at the Grand Duke's table were there primarily to be entertained, and it was the satirist's task to blend satire with humor, preferably almost unnoticeably. Beyond that, the satirist had to tread carefully, for some abuses are so central to a culture as not to lend themselves to satirical treatment. They must be dealt with seriously if they are dealt with at all, and a satirical treatment of them will lead to rejection of the entire work in which it is included.[7]

One of the most succinct statements from a Russian hand on the social importance of Neoclassical comedy was published quite late, in

1820, by Alexander Shakhovskoy (1777–1846), a prolific though now-forgotten playwright of the early nineteenth century. Comedy's task, he wrote then, is to take up where the laws leave off, to punish vice and raise moral standards. It may be true that comedies do not convert misers, but neither do laws. Miserly individuals do not enjoy being tagged with literary catch phrases, and many of the types satirized in Fonvizin's *Minor*, he wrote, are no longer with us. This socially beneficial action of comedy explains why wise rulers have always supported the theater from ancient times.[8] This latter point of Shakhovskoy's is buttressed by the fact that even Catherine—who certainly had the option of employing legislation if she wished— chose to combat certain social evils by writing satire herself.

If such nineteenth-century critics as Belinsky and Dudyshkin believed that Fonvizin had failed to weld satire and humor into an artistic comedy in *The Brigadier*, the theater-going public of the eighteenth century and critics of the twentieth felt otherwise. Though *The Brigadier* has its artistic weaknesses, and the author is not always in control of it, it stands as a skillful blend of humor and satire, in the best Fonvizinian style.

The Brigadier also has close connections with the Neoclassical tradition of comedy-writing, as well as Neoclassical satire.

Fonvizin's plotting of the play probably derived more from the Neoclassical farce than the Neoclassical comedy. This can be seen in the intermeshing marital triangles, and most especially in the repeated slapstick of the interruptions which intervene each time one of the male characters is on the point of pressing his illegitimate suit with the object of his affections. A Soviet student of eighteenth-century Russian literature, Grigory Gukovsky, has written that the structure of *The Brigadier* recalls the Sumarokovian Neoclassical farce, with its "gallery of comic personalities."[9] Another Soviet specialist, L. G. Barag, has fruitfully applied that insight by commenting that Fonvizin and his Western contemporaries developed the Molière tradition, achieving a new and organic synthesis of "elements of drama, comedy, and farce."[10] This interpretation of both Fonvizin's classic plays enables us to deal with their purely humorous aspects (the entertainment of farce), the moral guidance which they offered (the cleansing action of satire), and the near-tragic elements which critics have detected in such a figure as the Brigadier's wife (the drama). *The Brigadier* was neither pure entertainment nor pure didacticism, but a combination of the two, and with a dramatic element added.

In addition, Fonvizin did measure society against an ideal, and in the best Neoclassical tradition offered examples of that ideal. In fact, this is probably the most significant traditional element of the Neoclassical comedy which he retains, for his positive heroes Sofya and Dobrolyubov are indeed rather schematic, as the canons of Neoclassicism require. As Gukovsky phrases it in a formulation which is too sweeping for Fonvizin's comedy as a whole, but which does apply to his positive characters, "Fonvizin most often constructs his characters, not according to a rule of individual personality, but according to a previously conceived and limited scheme of moral and social norms."[11] Sofya and Dobrolyubov exist in order to demonstrate what is possible in a world in which virtue triumphs.

Another element of the Neoclassical tradition worth mention here is that of borrowing from literary predecessors. Even in modern literatures the line between direct borrowing and working within a tradition or current fashion may be a fine one, and we do well to remember that originality was not sought in medieval literature: since literature was so closely allied to Christian theology, an author was well advised *not* to be very original, for otherwise he could be accused of heresy. Fonvizin's work still retains some linkages with that Old Russian tradition (his tribute on the occasion of Grand Duke Paul's recovery, for instance, or the biography of Panin, reminiscent of Old Russian lives of the saints), and certainly he was within the Neoclassical tradition, which came near to approving of borrowing. Writing some fifty years later, when a great change had occurred in attitudes toward literary borrowings, Vyazemsky accused his subject several times of plagiarism (though not in *The Brigadier*), which he considered a very serious charge. Almost certainly a careful investigation of contemporary dramatic works would discover parallels with Fonvizin's first original play, and Strycek has demonstrated that Fonvizin lifted almost verbatim a passage in the conversation between the Brigadier and his son Ivanushka at the beginning of the third act from a play by Johann Christophe Gottsched.[12] It is significant, though, that this borrowing is connected with the highly stereotyped figure of the Gallomane, as is another play from which Fonvizin has been accused of borrowing, Holberg's *Jean de France*. Fonvizin never dealt with the question of his borrowings explicitly, but if he had, he might well have answered as did Shakovskoy in 1820 on the same subject. Shakhovskoy began by restating the Neoclassical tenet that art should deal with that which is common to all people at all times in all places:

Art . . . is not something which is conditional, depending on circumstances and fashion. . . . It is derived from the intellectual Nature of man, based on the lofty truths of morality and social justice, and therefore precise, unchanging, eternal.

From this it follows, Shakhovskoy continued, that writers should be prepared to take good things wherever they find them. Molière himself borrowed; I in turn borrowed from him; and I hope that in the future someone may borrow from me as well.[13] The Neoclassical approach did not go so far as to justify utter plagiarism, of course, but writers within the Neoclassical tradition were ready to countenance a much larger element of borrowing than was Vyazemsky in the nineteenth century, or we are today—although even in the twentieth century, when a writer develops a formula or plot which strikes a responsive chord among readers, hosts of literary imitators ring changes on that formula as quickly as possible.

III   *The Characters*

If we classify the personages of *The Brigadier* according to the degree of their abstraction, we see that, in addition to Sofya and Dobrolyubov, the Counsellor, the Counsellor's wife, and Ivanushka are primarily stock figures of Neoclassical comedy adapted to Russian conditions. The Counsellor recalls Molière's Tartuffe, the religious hypocrite who lusts after another man's wife while exuding a fog of ecclesiastical verbiage. Ivanushka is a nearly perfect specimen of the Russian Gallomane, who despises his backward parents who understand only Russian, and speaks a horrendous mixture of French and Russian. The Counselor's wife is a mixture of the giddy female spendthrift and the fashionable devotee of all things French, an aspect of her character which explains her attraction to Ivanushka, although he is considerably her junior. It is significant that the older generation have no proper names, even first names. They are defined solely by their stations in life, as the Brigadier, the Counselor's wife, and so forth. The representatives of the younger generation do bear proper names, but they are the most ordinary ones imaginable, and Dobrolyubov's name falls into the Neoclassical tradition of "speaking names," or names which define the essence of the character who bears them.

If most of the characters in *The Brigadier* are still clearly rooted in an internationalist Neoclassicism, the two most memorable ones are visibly joined to the Russian milieu in which they have their being. The Brigadier and the Brigadier's wife are expressions of Russian *byt*, or milieu. There is some disagreement over which of these two is the more remarkable. Nikita Panin immediately singled out the Brigadier's wife as the play's most vital and full-blooded creation: she was "everybody's relative," he said, and every Russian knew someone like her (II, 98–99). Thus it is understandable that, according to indirect evidence, the play may at one time have been entitled *Brigadir i brigadirsha* (The Brigadier and the Brigadier's Wife). [14] And yet Fonvizin in the end stubbornly called the play *The Brigadier*, and created the Brigadier as the only character lacking any important elements of caricature, the one with the greatest modicum of common sense, the one who usually recognizes the idiocy of those around him.

If the Brigadier and his wife were linked with native Russian culture, so was the ambiance of the play's action. The stage directions are detailed, calling for a room "decorated in rural fashion" and prescribing the initial activities 'and the dress of each of the major characters, who are all brought together for the important first scene. In his study of eighteenth-century Russian comedy, David Welsh claims that earlier plays had been quite featureless in their settings, and that therefore "its setting alone made *Brigadir* a startling novelty to the audiences of the 1760s and 1770s." [15] That may be true, but much of the play's interest was located in its "gallery of types," as several critics have commented.

To be sure, Sofya and Dobrolyubov are of interest, not as individualized characters, but rather in the context of the overall theme of the play, which will be discussed below. Consequently they are only very pale members of the "portrait gallery."

The Brigadier's wife, on the other hand, is a much more enthralling character, although she is so unintelligent that she cannot be psychologically very complex. She has the misfortune of being married to a man who enjoys denigrating her better qualities, who belittles her so that she has almost become a henpecked wife. In the very first scene of the first act, when the Counsellor comments that his daughter may be "losing her mind" a bit just before her imminent wedding, the Brigadier replies:

Oh, that will pass. My wife was walking around for about ten days out of her head before our marriage, and now she's been living with me for about thirty years afterwards in such perfect mental health that nobody could tell that she had ever been more intelligent. (I, 49)

His wife returns a weak rejoinder to her overbearing husband, but he has by now become quite accustomed to expressing his contempt for her. Late in the fourth act he unwittingly insults the Counsellor by assuring him that his wife would never betray him; and moreover, he scoffs, "The idiot hasn't yet been born who would ever get the notion of paying court to my wife" (I, 92). He rephrases that thought in several different ways, much to the Counsellor's rising disgust.

The reader need not rely merely upon the Brigadier's word for his wife's stupidity, for it is illustrated several times during the play. On a minor occasion, she cannot follow the rules of a new and more complicated game of cards which the others sit down to play. In her day card games were simpler, she says, and she did not have to command an entire specialized vocabulary in order to participate (I, 87). Her native denseness plays an important part in the humorous scene in which the Counsellor declares his love for her and attempts to seduce her. She would have been slow enough to comprehend even if her suitor had been more direct in his approach, for she believes in the traditional verities of marriage (her husband is right about that); but when in addition the Counsellor couches his intimations in indirect and elevated ecclesiastical language, the Brigadier's wife fails utterly to comprehend what is transpiring. In scene three of Act Two, when the Counsellor is finally alone with the Brigadier's wife, he approaches from a distance by bewailing his sins and complaining of the drastic steps he would have to take if he genuinely wished to be rid of them—which he does not. When the Brigadier's wife questions him about these "sins," he explains:

Counsellor: . . . Every man is composed of body and spirit. The spirit indeed may be willing, but the flesh is weak. And then there is no sin which cannot be purified through repentance . . . (*Tenderly*) Let us sin and then repent.
Brigadier's wife: How can we not sin, uncle! God alone is without sin.
Counsellor: True, dear woman. And you yourself confess now that you have known this sin.
Brigadier's wife: I always make my confession, uncle, the first week of Lent. But tell me, what need have you of my sins?
Counsellor: I have exactly the same need of your sins as I do of salvation. I wish your sins and mine to be one and the same so that nothing can dissolve the conjunction of our bodies and souls.

Brigadier's wife: What on earth do you mean by conjunction, uncle? I don't understand church language any better than I do French. (I, 65)

The Counsellor is thus frustrated by the incomprehension of the Brigadier's wife, who realizes what has occurred when her son and the Counsellor's wife explain it to her. Then she can only with difficulty be restrained from causing a scandal by denouncing the Counsellor to her husband (I, 66–67).

The Brigadier also blames his wife for having botched the job of raising their son. Every time he wanted to subject his son to some military discipline, the Brigadier says, the mother always objected: "What do you want to do with the poor infant?" (I, 75). And now we see the results of that indulgence: "His idiot mother," the Brigadier declares, "and my wife, is the reason he became a rake, and even a French rake, the more's the pity" (I, 90). The Brigadier will, in short, accept no responsibility for what his son has become.

The Brigadier does not restrict his hostility toward his wife to verbal abuse; he sometimes mistreats her physically as well. At the very beginning of the fourth act she comes in to complain to Sofya and Dobrolyubov, to solicit their solace and perhaps protection. Knowing her husband's "terrible temper," she fears again falling victim to it. Though she suffers greatly from her husband's brutality, she tells Sofya, other military wives had even greater trials to bear. Such was the case with the beautiful young wife of a certain captain Gvozdilov, she recalls, who, in drunken fits, constantly beat her within an inch of her life. The tender-minded Sofya cries out in horror and asks to hear no more, to which the Brigadier's wife replies: "Ah, my dear girl, you can't even stand to hear about it! What do you think it was like for the captain's wife?" (I, 84–85). And here the Brigadier's wife, for all her muddle-headedness, does move within the realm of tragedy. Nearly 100 years later Fedor Dostoevsky would single out this dialogue as a masterly dramatic vignette, and pay tribute to Fonvizin's artistic tact in giving the final word to the Brigadier's wife instead of to the "well brought up Sofya with her hothouse sensitivity." "This is an astounding piece of repartee . . . of Fonvizin's," the novelist declared, "and he never wrote anything more appropriate, more humane, and . . . more despairing."[16]

Probably the most complex and most intelligent character of the play is the Brigadier. He is also the most consistently developed, as the radical nineteenth-century critic Nikolay Chernyshevsky wrote

in a youthful essay otherwise quite hostile to Fonvizin's play.[17]
Certainly he is the work's most "realistic" creation.

The Brigadier is not a particularly positive character. A military
man, he is rough, rather crude, and given to physical violence: at one
point in the play he nearly comes to blows with his son. He is on
several occasions accused of being crude to his son—especially by the
Counsellor's wife—and to his wife, by the Counsellor, who
rationalizes his own lecherous coveting of his neighbor's wife by
arguing that the Brigadier "sometimes doesn't love his wife as much
as he does his horse" (I, 64). In addition to being crude and
straightforward, the Brigadier is also something of a cynic, and his
contempt for both his wife and son blinds him to the reality of what is
occurring under his nose. In the opening scene of Act Three, for
instance, he upbraids Ivanushka for his Gallomania, and makes a
critical comment which his son misinterprets as a compliment. His
father thereupon explodes: "You're a real blockhead, aren't you?
Here I call you an idiot and you think I'm flattering you: what a jackass
you are!" (I, 72). Precisely this disregard for his son makes it difficult
for him to comprehend that the Counsellor's wife really prefers
Ivanushka to him, even though she clearly demonstrates her preference to him both in word and deed. When he finally realizes the true
situation, he expresses his disillusion through cynicism about women, as when he remarks to the Counsellor that "women usually
maintain their chastity with worthwhile men, but very rarely with
playboys" (I, 93). Here he has himself in mind as a worthwhile man,
and his son as the playboy.

Still, the Brigadier is not averse to coveting his neighbor's wife,
either, and makes his declaration to the Counsellor's wife in another
rather comic scene. Just as the Counsellor utilizes ecclesiastical
terminology, so the Brigadier resorts to military vocabulary in
pressing his case. Facing her charms is more frightening to him than
moving forward on the battlefield, he declares: "Your eyes are more
terrifying to me than any bullets, shell, and shrapnel. Their first
volley pierced my heart through and through, but before they plug
me, I'll surrender as your prisoner of war" (I, 80). Like the Brigadier's
wife, the Counsellor's wife at least pretends not to understand her
unwanted suitor's intentions, and puts him off.

Slowly the Brigadier realizes the true state of affairs, and during the
climactic scene when all the intertwining intrigues are exposed, it is
in his mouth that Fonvizin places his favorite phrase, "honest man."
"Ivan, have the carriage brought around," he orders. "Wife, let us

this very minute leave a house where I, an honest man, almost became a ne'er-do-well" (I, 102). His decisive action scarcely redeems him entirely, but it does point to a certain rough honesty in him which was nearly eclipsed in the hypocritical atmosphere of the Counsellor's home.

The fount of that hypocrisy is the Counsellor. His wife says of him (we might note generally that each of the four spouses analyzes his partner reasonably accurately): "My freak is a terrible hypocrite: he never misses either morning or evening services, and thinks . . . God is so complacent as to forgive him during an evening service for what he has stolen during the day" (I, 55). Sometimes the Counsellor attempts to deceive even himself by his moral rationalizations. He was forced into retirement from government service upon the passage of strict legislation against bribery, and at one point he complains to his daughter about the new order of things under which one must be found guilty before paying a penalty: in God's eyes, he argues, all have sinned, and in his day as a judge "the guilty used to pay for his guilt and the innocent for his innocence . . . and so everyone was satisfied" (I, 61).

On the other hand, occasionally the Counsellor does understand the essentials of Christian ethics sufficiently to comprehend his offenses. In a monologue in the second scene of Act Two, he bewails his sins in attempting to seduce another man's wife, and also in using his paternal authority to compel his daughter to marry against her wishes, so that he himself may enjoy ready access to the Brigadier's wife. He bewails his sins but nevertheless acts in a way he knows to be wrong, so that he is the most actively evil character in the play.

Sofya sets out the essence of her father's character correctly when—after Dobrolyubov has won his suit and become a man of means—she says that her father's permission for their marriage will depend upon whether his greed overcomes his love (I, 83). Consequently, it is appropriate that at the end the Counsellor should be the person whose evil plans have been most thoroughly thwarted, and it is to him that the play's concluding moral message is given: "They say it's difficult to live with a conscience: but now I've discovered myself that the worst thing in the world is to live without one" (I, 103). The Counsellor stands exposed as the hypocrite who presents a facade of morality to the world while actually living an unworthy life.

There is little to be said about either Ivanushka or the Counsellor's wife as personalities. Ivanushka has inherited his mother's lack of wit, although he is shrewd enough to camouflage that failing with fashionable phrases. The Counsellor's wife is a spendthrift who loves taking three hours of a morning at her toilet and dreams of receiving hats in the latest fashion from Moscow from time to time (I, 55–56). This addlepated pair are the embodiment of Gallomania, which is one of the play's principal themes.

IV *Structure and Themes*

The superficial observer might consider *The Brigadier* primarily an assault upon Gallomania, and with some justification. The stock characters of Ivanushka and the Counsellor's wife are simultaneously vivid and flat, and so quite memorable; the passages dealing with Gallomania are both comical and scattered throughout the play, so that they easily imprint themselves upon the memory. However, Marvin Kantor, after making a detailed comparison of *The Brigadier* with Holberg's *Jean de France*, concludes correctly that Fonvizin's play must not be pigeonholed in such cavalier fashion:

Holberg's comedy is what might be termed a "monolithic" satire, i.e., a satire which is uniformly singular throughout: one theme, one hero, one target, etc. [Gallomania]. Fonvizin's work, in complete contrast, is what might be termed a "composite" satire, i.e., a satire which is manifoldly plural throughout: several themes, several heroes, several targets, etc. As a result, his play is a generalized picture of the social morals and manners of Russia's noble society of the time.[18]

The Gallomania of Ivanushka and the Counsellor's wife is introduced quite early, in the first scene of the first act, when Ivanushka comments that he would much prefer a wife with whom he could speak only French (I, 48). Ivanushka and the Counsellor's wife both employ French constantly, inserting whole phrases and sentences into their Russian as well as French grammatical calques, or utilizing individual words in some Russian transformation, much to the discomfort of the others, who know no French. The attachment of the Gallomane to France is not just linguistic, but also cultural, in the bad sense: the Russian Gallomanes have adopted, not the worthwhile elements of French culture, but its fashionable idiocies. For example, the primary love scene between Ivanushka and the Counsellor's wife is conducted in the language of cards and card-playing, in Fonvizin's view something of a cultural plague imported from France along with most of its terminology. When the Counsellor's wife tells

Ivan of his father's advances, he proposes to challenge his father to a duel. When his beloved demurs, he replies:

Et pourquoi non? I read in an excellent book, what was the title . . . *le nom m'est echappé* . . . yes, in the book *Les Sottises du temps*, that a son in Paris once challenged his father to a duel . . . or am I such a swine as not to imitate what has happened even once in Paris? (I, 70)

Shortly thereafter, during a dispute with his father, Ivanushka proudly declares that his body may have been born in Russia, but his spirit belongs to the French crown (I, 72). This remark points to a vital corollary of the Gallomane's love for France, that is, his hatred for Russia. Ivan's chief ambition is to abandon his native land and become an inhabitant of France. He complains bitterly that it is impossible for a Russian ever to forget completely the fact of his birth (I, 78). Toward the end of the play, in a passage which some critics have considered out of character, Ivanushka remarks that he has come to hate all things Russian because he was educated by a "French coachman." "A young person is like wax," he says. "If, *malheureuse-ment,* I had had a Russian who loved his own country as a tutor, perhaps I would not be what I am" (I, 98). It is this denationalization which Fonvizin finds most reprehensible in the superficial admirers of France. In his travel writings of a decade later he would argue that it was perfectly possible to absorb the positive aspects of French culture without at the same time negating one's native culture. But the superficial Gallomanes were simply ridiculous, and Fonvizin made them the butt of his memorable satire.

Ivanushka's remark about his denationalized upbringing points to yet another important theme within the play, that of the education of the young. This theme was central to Russian satire throughout the century, beginning in Peter's time, when the state set about educating the young by compulsion if necessary; Fonvizin would develop it in more detail in *The Minor*.

The Russian word involved here is *vospitanie*, or general upbringing, a term with different connotations than *obrazovanie*, or education in the more strictly intellectual sense. The members of the older generation in *The Brigadier* are indifferent, even hostile, to purely intellectual training. In the play's very first scene the Counsellor urges Ivanushka to apply himself to reading. When the young man asks what he should read, each older person proposes things from his limited and practical experience: the Brigadier suggests military regulations; the Counsellor, laws and decrees; the Brigadier's wife,

account books; and the Counsellor's wife, romantic novels (I, 48–49).
When it comes to such impractical things as the study of grammar, all
four members of the older generation agree that they have lived their
lives perfectly well without any knowledge of grammar whatever (I,
52–53).

More essential than intellectual discipline is the moral training of
the young. Here the Brigadier and his wife have failed abysmally,
although—quite inconsistently—the Counsellor and his wife are
blessed with an absolutely ideal daughter. Nothing can convince the
Brigadier's wife that her son is anything but highly intelligent; she is
overprotective, and spoils him at every turn, as her husband rightly
complains. In return, unfortunately, she receives nothing but contempt; her son is even bitter about the fact that his parents are still
alive. The case of Ivanushka and his progenitors stimulates Dobrolyubov to generalize about the large number of children who do
their parents "dishonor," and to explain, without elaborating, that
the cause of all this is *vospitanie* (I, 90). In a sense, then, Fonvizin
blames the older generation for the shortcomings of the younger
generation: had the former raised them properly, the latter would not
have turned out so badly.

And that is linked to the most basic theme of the play, which is the
ideal of the family and family relationships, most especially between
husband and wife, but also between parents and children. The
families of the older generation caricature that ideal, while the
prospective family of Sofya and Dobrolyubov upholds it. The kernel
of this notion is articulated in the concluding scene of the first act,
when Sofya and Dobrolyubov discuss the complicated situation
which has come into being by this time. Sofya remarks that everyone
seems to be in love except the Brigadier's wife, to which Dobrolyubov replies: "That's true, but the difference is that their love is
ridiculous and shameful and does them dishonor, while our love is
based upon honorable intentions and is such that everyone should
desire our happiness" (I, 59–60). The idea is sententiously phrased,
but the meaning is clear. The love of Sofya and Dobrolyubov and
their conception of the family are contrasted in every possible way
with those of the negative characters in the play.

First of all, marriage should be based upon mutual love, and not
upon other considerations, such as money in the case of the Counsellor, or prestige, as in the case of the Brigadier. Initially it appears that
Dobrolyubov may lose all he has, since his estate is tied up in a

lawsuit, but Sofya assures him that his financial status will not affect her love for him (I, 60). He ends up quite well off, however, and that does not affect her feeling for him either. In the second place, parents should not arrange marriages against the wishes of their children. The Counsellor unjustly seeks to exert his parental authority over his daughter, who resists strongly but who might possibly have married according to his instructions and against her inclination (I, 62–63). Ivan's mother also pressures him to go through with the marriage even though he has not chosen his bride, as she recalls how things were in the old days: when she married, she says, "we had never even heard of each other. I never said a word to him before the wedding, and I only began to talk with him a wee bit a couple of weeks after the wedding" (I, 96). But it is precisely the example of his parents' relationship which has altogether soured Ivanushka on the idea of marriage, or so he claims. The proper marriage, as the play demonstrates, is made when each partner freely chooses the other, and both receive the free agreement of their parents.

Within marriage, relations between husband and wife should be guided by mutual love and respect. This principle is totally ignored by the Counsellor's wife, who regularly terms her husband a "freak" *(urod);* by the Brigadier, who constantly belittles his wife; and by the Counsellor, who detests his wife's flightiness. To be sure, the Counsellor understands in theory what a good marriage should be: his wife says he believes that "husband and wife comprise one person" (I, 97), and he extends the notion of family unity to different generations when he tells Sofya that "a father and his children should think alike" (I, 61). He also upholds the traditional idea of the husband as general head of the family, with the wife subordinate. When Sofya objects that Ivanushka has "not the least respect" for her, he replies: "What sort of respect do you want from him? It seems to me that you should respect him, and not he you. He will be your head, and not you his" (I, 62). Such formulations as these make it plain that the Counsellor uses the traditional concepts of the family merely to justify his own domestic despotism over his wife and daughter.

In the final accounting the victory goes to the traditional concept of the family, but a concept now infused with moral content and cleansed from false historical accretions. Dobrolyubov and Sofya marry according to their mutual affection, with parental approval. Husband and wife will be one flesh, and the husband the final authority in the family, but he will always consult his wife on any matter of mutual concern. Husband and wife will be faithful to each other (at one point Ivanushka is upset to hear that Sofya would be a "constant" wife, for that would be totally unfashionable [I, 56–67]), conjoined by a true and spiritual love as contrasted with the animal lust which drives the older generation to its infidelities.

Although some critics have thought otherwise, *The Brigadier* is rather skillfully constructed, except for the fourth act, which wanders and seems to have been written largely to flesh out the obligatory Neoclassical five acts. The first scene of Act One brings all the characters with the exception of Dobrolyubov together immediately, and establishes many of the interrelationships between them. The act ends with the conversation between Sofya and Dobrolyubov which sets the stage for the ultimate fulfillment of their love. Each remaining act begins with a dialogue between two major characters which explores their mutual relationships: Act Two starts with the Counsellor and his daughter; Act Three, with the Brigadier and his son; Act Four, briefly, with Sofya and Dobrolyubov; and Act Five, with Ivan and his mother. In the second and third acts the man who begins by admonishing his son or daughter then makes advances to another man's wife, while the relationship between Ivanushka and the Counsellor's wife is dealt with in each of the first three acts. The fourth act serves as a transition to Act Five, in which all the chief characters are gradually brought together—as they were at the beginning of the first act—and the denouement ensues.

The Brigadier exerted a considerable impact upon its times. A blend of farce, comedy, and drama, it amused audiences with a substantial element of straight slapstick and humor, especially in the relations of Ivanushka with the Counsellor's wife. It also dealt with serious contemporary questions, particularly those of the ideal of the family, the upbringing of the young, and Gallomania. Not limiting itself to criticism, it sketched a positive ideal in the figures of Sofya and Dobrolyubov. Its language, especially in the dialogue of the Brigadier's wife with its many elements of folk speech, was new, humorous, and interesting.

The Brigadier has its faults, which some critics have even overemphasized. Chernyshevsky wrote that he did a little counting, and out of every eleven pages found only one good one as opposed to ten poor or mediocre ones.[19] But such critics apply an illegitimate yardstick to the play, for they have the experience of the first half of the nineteenth century behind them. Critics like Nikita Panin, though amateurs, were still well acquainted with the state of Russian comedy before 1769, and therefore were "not surprised that this comedy had had such success" (II, 99). Now, more than two centuries later, the play retains most of its vitality.

CHAPTER 4

The Minor

I *Preliminary Considerations*

Nedorosl' (The Minor) is the work which brought Fonvizin literary immortality. It is virtually the only eighteenth-century play included in the repertory of contemporary theaters in the Soviet Union; indeed, it may be regarded as *the* classic work of eighteenth-century Russian literature in the sense that the nonspecialist Russian is more likely to have read it than any other work of that period. In the Soviet Union of today, it is frequently reprinted, though nearly always with an appropriate essay interpreting it as a work of Critical Realism laying bare the social injustices rampant in Russia at the height of Catherine's reign. To some degree the play does sustain such an interpretation.

Its major characters divide into two groups, positive and negative. The negative characters include the Prostakov family (the name is derived from the word for "simpleton"). The leading figure in the family is the petty domestic tyrant Mrs. Prostakova, who terrifies her family and servants by her obstreperous temper. The rest of the family consists of her henpecked husband, Mr. Prostakov; her dullard son Mitrofan, whose name indicates by its Greek roots that he is created in the likeness of his mother; and her coarse brother Skotinin, who prefers the company of swine to that of humans.

Mitrofan is the *nedorosl'* of the title: a young man who has not yet reached his majority of fifteen years. Rather strict legislation promulgated by Peter the Great early in the century had forbidden young noblemen to marry until they had completed their education and were no longer "minors." Like so many noble boys of the period, Mitrofan was educated at home, in this case by three tutors: Tsyfirkin, a retired soldier who attempts to teach his charge mathematics; Kuteykin, a seminary student engaged to give instruction in theology, philosophy, grammar, and related subjects; and

Vralman, a German who speaks heavily accented Russian and is totally without qualifications as a tutor since he had previously been a coachman. But Mitrofan is incapable of benefiting even from such teachers as these, and says, in one of the play's most famous phrases, "I don't want to study, I want to get married." Thereon hangs the plot.

The young lady at the center of the play's marital intrigues is the Prostakovs' ward, Sofya, whom Mrs. Prostakova initially plans to marry off to her brother Skotinin. Just before that engagement is fixed, however, Sofya receives a letter from her uncle, Starodum, long thought dead but now in Moscow, announcing his impending visit to the Prostakov estate. Starodum also informs Sofya that she will be his heir, and that piece of information abruptly alters Mrs. Prostakova's attitude toward her. She now decides that Sofya should go to Mitrofan rather than to her brother.

Sofya—who is obviously out of place in the Prostakov household—serves as the link between the negative group of characters and the positive ones, headed by Starodum and by Pravdin (his name derives from *pravda,* "justice"), who represents governmental authority. Another important positive figure is Sofya's beloved Milon, an officer who conveniently arrives in the town commanding a detachment of soldiers and initially unaware of Sofya's whereabouts. Both Milon and Sofya wish to be joined in marriage, and obtain Starodum's assent to their marriage after a time.

Prostakova, realizing that the projected marriage between Mitrofan and Sofya is about to fall through, plots to abduct Sofya and force her into the marriage. Milon foils the plot, and retribution visits the Prostakov family: when Mrs. Prostakova sets out to punish the servants who had bungled the abduction, Pravdin produces a decree depriving her of all her authority and property in the name of the state, on the grounds that she has consistently abused her serfs. At the end even her son turns against her, and she is stripped of everything she had thought important. "Such are the appropriate fruits of immorality," says Starodum in the play's concluding sentence, pointing to the despairing woman.

We know considerably less about the composition of *The Minor* than we do about *The Brigadier*. One hotly disputed question about its genesis has to do with a manuscript first published only in 1933 (and included in an appendix to Makogonenko's 1959 edition of Fonvizin), generally known as the "early" *Minor*. A number of

Fonvizin specialists, including most recently Strycek, accept this work as Fonvizin's and believe it to have been written probably in the mid-1760s.[1] Other scholars deny that this work is a preliminary version of *The Minor*. The Soviet specialist A.P. Mogilyansky, for instance, after exhaustively investigating the manuscripts of the "Early Version," concludes they were written in the middle or later 1770s, probably by someone associated with the circle of Denis Fonvizin's brother Pavel.[2] In a special appendix to his study of Fonvizin, K.V. Pigarev maintains that the "Early Version" was written as an imitation of *The Minor* very soon after it appeared on stage or in print.[3] The fact that the plays bear the same title means there must be some connection between them. However, the two plays have entirely different casts of characters, with quite different names; the aesthetic worth of the "Early Version" is very low indeed. Consequently, Pigarev's hypothesis seems most nearly correct. The "Early Version" is so helpless as literature that it is difficult to believe it could have been written by Fonvizin even at a very early age; and if Mogilyansky is correct in asserting that the manuscript could not have been produced before the middle 1770s, then Fonvizin's authorship is virtually excluded. The "Early Version" was most probably produced by some anonymous and quite untalented individual as one of the first of the play's numerous imitations.

The first concrete information about the work's composition at our disposal is found in an unpublished letter of July 11, 1779, which reports Fonvizin to be "writing a comedy with great success."[4] Beyond this we know very little about the writer's progress on the play until its completion in January or February of 1782 and its premiere performance in St. Petersburg on September 24 of that year.[5] Although the play was released anonymously—as were most of the other original literary works Fonvizin issued, for some reason—the theater-going public knew very well who had created it. The early nineteenth-century literary historian Metropolitan Evgeny Bolkhovitinov—who was not always especially accurate in recording dates and places—noted that Potemkin had summoned Fonvizin after its first staging and uttered the famous sentence: "You should die now, Denis, or never write anything else: your name will be immortal because of this one play." The quote may be apocryphal, for Pavel Berkov points out that Potemkin could not have attended the St. Petersburg premiere of 1782; but he adds that perhaps Potemkin made the comment at an earlier reading of the play, and even assisted in having it staged.[6] However that may be, the phrase *Umri Denis*

(You should die now, Denis) has attached itself to *The Minor*, and to Fonvizin, in literary folklore. Certainly it accurately, if a bit hyperbolically, gauged the work's importance for the Russian theater and for Fonvizin's career.

Having *The Minor* staged in Moscow was a matter of some difficulty. Immediately after the St. Petersburg premiere the author wrote a letter in French (II, 496–97) to Michael Maddox, an itinerant English showman who had come to Russia in 1776 and by 1780 established a Moscow theater, which burned down in 1806.[7] The Moscow censor must have hindered the play's staging there. Fonvizin was anxious to see his play performed in his native city, but also quite worried that he would be identified as its author: he enjoined Maddox not to let the manuscript out of his possession, since he "did not yet want to give it any publicity."

Fonvizin's hopes for a Moscow premiere were fulfilled on May 18, 1783. Soon *The Minor* was setting the pace for the Russian theater of its day. An indication of this was the relative rapidity with which it began to be translated into foreign languages. While in Austria for his health in 1787, Fonvizin described a pleasant May morning spent listening to a reading of the German translation of his play in the company of some attractive German ladies that must have been a tonic for him in his enfeebled condition (II, 570). Scholars were unable to locate this particular translation for many years, until in 1958 one discovered a copy in the Lenin Library in Moscow. Entitled *Das Muttersöhnchen,* the translation was published in Leipzig and Vienna in 1787 (Vralman, incidentally, had been transformed into a Frenchman).[8] Subsequently the work was translated into numerous European languages.

The impact of *The Minor* upon the literature of its time may be measured in other ways as well. In a major study of Russian comedy of the eighteenth century, perhaps the greatest prerevolutionary specialist on Russian literature of that period, Vasily Sipovsky, divided the considerable number of plays written between 1785 and 1800 into three major categories. The first of these comprised imitations of *The Minor*, sometimes with the same characters.[9] The Soviet scholar L.G. Barag has done the rather dreary work of perusing an entire series of now-forgotten plays of the period which were based on *The Minor*. He traces, for example, a descendant of Starodum in the character of Pravomysl from Nikolay Emin's *Mnimyi mudrets* (The Imaginary Philosopher) of 1787, and identifies a sequel to Fonvizin's play in the anonymous *Mitrofanushkiny imeniny* (Mitrofan's Nameday) of 1807.[10] These and many other imitations demonstrate that *The Minor* created a certain literary school, even though Fonvizin himself engendered few direct imitators. The literary quality of the "school" was very low and none of the plays has survived as anything more than an obscure footnote to literary history, but their very existence demonstrates that *The Minor* cut a swath through the Russian theater for a quarter-century or more. That is an impressive achievement for any single literary work.

There were those who thought the play severely distorted reality. In his study of Fonvizin Pigarev cites two early nineteenth-century articles whose authors protested that such "eccentrics" as the ones Fonvizin depicted in his play had never existed in real life.[11] This raises the ultimately unresolvable question of the "realism" of a literary work and the "typicality" of its characters, a question the more difficult to settle at a remove of two centuries. If some indignant critics of that day wrote that the monstrously negative characters of the play never could have existed, more modern ones tend to believe that such idealized figures as Starodum and Pravdin could have had no basis in contemporary reality. Yet others argue that both groups were drawn from life and were completely realistic. Vyazemsky, for instance, recognized the element of caricature in Fonvizin's art and attempted to salvage his "Realism" in an ingenious manner. "The portrait painter," he wrote, "idealizes his original slightly for an artistic purpose; the master caricaturist idealizes his original in a humorous and distorted way; but they both are faithful to the truth,"[12] that is, they both remain linked to reality. One may speculate how far a writer might stray from reality under such a formula, but any writer clearly requires some such flexibility.

As it happens, Fonvizin himself is of aid in considering the problem of typicality. Although we know of no particular prototypes for the heroes of *The Minor*, in years following the play's publication Fonvizin encountered one or two actually existing persons who confirmed the precision of his artistic intuition. He records the most striking instance of this in his journal for May 24, 1786, when, on their way to Austria, the Fonvizins lodged in a provincial Russian town with a certain couple who were "genuine Prostakovs" (II, 565). Fonvizin even had some things to say about the most blatantly caricatured personage of his play, Skotinin, that adept of swinishness. In late 1784 Fonvizin and his wife arrived in a small Italian town, where they took the best available accommodations. They were poor enough, though. "In our room," he wrote, ". . . there was dreadful filth and dirt, worse than there ever would be in my Skotinin's pigsties, of course" (II, 537). The almost affectionate manner in which Skotinin's creator refers to him is revealing, and fits with the information that in early 1784 Fonvizin played the role of Skotinin at least once when the play was staged.[13] Such a jocular attitude indicates that Fonvizin would hardly have shared the opinion of some later critics that his comic figures were moral monstrosities capable of inspiring the deepest revulsion in the beholder. For Fonvizin they were relatively harmless, though undesirable; in the Russian nineteenth-century tradition they occupied the same place as, say, some of Charles Dickens's characters in the English literary tradition of a later period.

If this is so, we must regard with considerable skepticism the interpretation placed upon *The Minor* by the influential historian Vasily Klyuchevsky in an article devoted entirely to the play.[14] Klyuchevsky worries about recommending *The Minor* as reading for young people, for, he says, the "humorous" characters are not funny, and the virtuous ones are not lifelike. "All these," he maintains, "are the false notes, not of a comedy, but of the way of life depicted in it. This comedy is an incomparable mirror." According to Klyuchevsky, *The Minor* is a grim portrait of the Russian life of its time, and not at all the humorous entertainment piece of the standard literary textbooks. If Klyuchevsky was correct in berating—as he did—those who ignored the play's social significance, he committed an equivalent error in failing to recognize the literary, and specifically comic, elements of the play.

Despite his exaggerations, Klyuchevsky does point up an important consideration in the analysis of *The Minor*, one present embryonically in *The Brigadier*. That is the tragic, or serious, element in a work which is formally a comedy. Pigarev is correct in saying the play "provokes, not simple, merry laughter, but bitter laughter which causes one to meditate deeply."[15] Pavel Berkov urges that Mitrofan's role—certainly primarily a humorous one—should be played by an actor with "a grotesque, and not burlesque conception of this image," and not as farce.[16] The distinction between grotesque and burlesque is important here, for a burlesque lacks any deeper implications, whereas a grotesque points through bitter laughter to an ultimately serious reality. Vyazemsky had something of this sort in mind when he commented that, in the personage of Mrs. Prostakova, *The Minor* contains within itself the potential of tragedy.[17] Vyazemsky's sympathies tended to lie with the gentry class and Berkov's with the common people, which is why the latter once wrote that the servant Eremeevna—Mitrofan's nurse, who suffers unconscionably at Mrs. Prostakova's hands—was a "complete and classical type of an enslaved serf woman, uncomplaining, attached and devoted to those who torture her, and therefore a deeply tragic type."[18]

The tragic potentialities of *The Minor*—whether in Mrs. Prostakova, Mitrofan, or Eremeevna—are scarcely realized, however, or are realized only for fleeting moments. Consequently the play may be most appropriately defined either as a "tearful comedy" (*sleznaia komediia*),[19] or else as an instance of the so-called *genre sérieux*, or serious comedy, as the American investigator David Patterson has recently suggested.[20] Patterson points out that as early as 1757 Denis Diderot had begun formulating the notion of the *genre sérieux*, which combined "nuances from both comedy and tragedy," and in his *De la poésie dramatique* (1758) spoke of the "serious comedy, which has as its object virtue and the duties of man." A persuasive argument can be made that *The Minor* fits clearly into this category: though fundamentally a comedy, it has serious objectives in mind.

II   *The Negative Characters*

In *The Brigadier* the positive and negative characters are partially interconnected by blood, since the positive Sofya is the daughter of the wholly negative Counsellor. In *The Minor* Fonvizin carefully separates the positive from the negative characters, with Sofya as the chief point of contact between them. As a consequence, at the play's conclusion he can portray the opposition between good and evil very starkly.

The dominant figure of the negative camp in *The Minor* is Mrs. Prostakova: her son at one point defines himself as "my mother's son" and her husband at the same point as "my wife's husband" (I, 137), while Skotinin derives his standing in the play from his relationship to Mrs. Prostakova. She is the work's "evil fury," the person seemingly dominating the miniature world that was the Russian landed estate of the eighteenth and nineteenth centuries, when the landowner could handle things very much as he wished, without interference from the local or central governmental authorities. In large measure the estate was an independent economic entity which could manage indefinitely almost entirely cut off from the outside world. It is on such semi-independent estates that some of the greatest Russian literature is set, from the plays of Fonvizin to the novels of Ivan Turgenev.

Mrs. Prostakova brutalizes first of all her serfs, over whom she believes she has absolute power. She commonly addresses them as "swine" (*skot*), and exercises her power arbitrarily, as the first scene of the play makes clear. Here the tailor Trishka has been instructed to sew Mitrofan a coat, with which his mistress finds fault simply for the sake of finding fault, so as to make life miserable for Trishka. She claims that the coat is too tight, her husband thinks it too loose, and it seems to Skotinin to have been sewn quite properly, much to his sister's disgust. In the same manner Prostakova lords it over Eremeevna, paying her, as the house servant puts it, "five rubles a year and five slaps a day" (I, 128). On another occasion Prostakova flies into a rage when she learns that one of her servant girls is not only ill, but running a high fever and raving. "Raving, the beast!" she screams. "As if she were a noblewoman!" (I, 136).

Mrs. Prostakova is a quintessential bully, ready to lord it over her inferiors and equally prepared to grovel before her superiors. In the midst of the third act, upon first recognizing the newly arrived Starodum, she nearly loses her head:

What, is that you, our uncle!? Our precious guest! Oh, I'm an absolute idiot! Is this any way to greet our own father in whom we all hope, our only father, like a piece of dust in the eye? Uncle, please forgive me, I'm a fool. I just can't come to my senses. . . . (I, 136)

Starodum is properly contemptuous of this exercise in self-abasement for ulterior motives, and precisely this trait of her character triggers her downfall. For, once her scandalous abduction attempt has failed and she realizes she may lose a great deal, Mrs. Prostakova falls to her knees before all those whom she has offended in the most abject manner imaginable. She first seeks forgiveness of Sofya, who generously grants it, and then turns to Starodum, confessing that she is a "human being and no angel." Though initially Starodum is reluctant to excuse her, he soon yields to his better nature. But the word "forgive" has no sooner left his mouth than Prostakova springs to her feet, vowing vengeance upon her subordinates. At this point—rather as in the biblical story of the servant cast into debtors prison when, after his lord had forgiven him his debt, he would not do the same for those indebted to him—Pravdin intervenes with the full authority of the state, to complete Prostakova's humiliation.

Mrs. Prostakova's vices are sometimes distortions of potential virtues. Her own inhumanity to her servants she manages to interpret as flowing from her determination to manage the estate properly: "I simply work from dawn to dusk, wearing myself out swearing and beating people up; that's all that keeps the place going!" (I, 124). Another possible virtue transformed into a vice is her devotion to her unworthy son: "My only care and my only joy is Mitrofanushka," she says to the assembled guests on one occasion (I, 125). When she grew up, no attention at all was paid to education, but she prides herself on having provided her son with one regular tutor, Vralman, and two supplementary teachers. The distortion enters when she insists on overprotecting him. When he displays his ignorance, she excuses him by claiming he has overexerted himself, or that what he does not know is not worth knowing. Consequently she ends by raising an utter moral monster, created in her own image, and therefore without the slightest sense of obligation to her for what she has done for him. It is he who delivers the final blow to her shattered pride when, after she has lost her estate, he crudely rebuffs her as she turns to him for consolation (I, 177). Like his mother, Mitrofan is the epitome of pure selfishness, and in him Prostakova reaps the fruits of her misguided maternal love. Thus it is that attitudes and actions which might have been to her credit are instead twisted into instruments of her destruction.

Still, despite her evil personality, Prostakova is the play's most memorable character, the most individualized, the one who summarizes the meaning of the work for the ordinary reader.

Hardly less vivid than Prostakova is Skotinin. The Soviet scholar L. I. Kulakova remarks that the power of Prostakova's image lies precisely in the fact of her relative ordinariness: she was not a sadistic torturer of her serfs, like certain historical female landowners of the eighteenth century, but rather a "quite usual sort of woman landowner."[21] Though it is possible to make a plausible argument supporting this view, it is difficult to perceive Skotinin as anything other than a caricature. He is a former military man, so unintelligent that he had never risen very high in the ranks: as he says of himself, "If I once get something into my head, you can't get it out of there with a nail" (I, 120). One source of the play's conflict is the fact that Skotinin believes Sofya has been promised to him, and he does not appreciate competing with his nephew for her hand. But Skotinin desires Sofya, not for herself, but for the sake of her estates, on which there are a number of pigs, for Skotinin desires nothing more than pigs. In a brief speech to his sister with obvious applications beyond its literal meaning, Skotinin says: "I love pigs, my dear sister, and in our county we have such huge pigs that there's not a single one wouldn't be taller than any of us by a head if it stood up on its hind legs" (I, 112). When he learns of Sofya's inheritance, Skotinin's enthusiasm waxes: with her money he can "buy up all the pigs in this wide world" (I, 121). Some of his further remarks make it plain that swine are closer to his heart than any wife could be.

As the play progresses, Skotinin sees that his prize is slipping from his grasp, and his native greed engenders desperation. At one point he threatens his nephew with physical harm and even death if he persists in his suit (I, 122); at another he and his sister nearly fall to a hair-pulling fistfight over the cancellation of his marriage plans (I, 135). Here the situation becomes quite farcical, and the scene on stage is designed primarily for the audience's entertainment.

The crude Skotinin is basically a comic character, although he also exhibits in extreme form the source of the negative characteristics of Prostakova and of Mitrofan: on one occasion Skotinin comments that Mitrofan also likes pigs, and the long-suffering Prostakov agrees that there is a point of resemblance there (I, 112).

Mr. Prostakov plays a relatively unimportant role in *The Minor*. In one of his aspects he is the typical repressed husband: in scene three of Act One, when the sewing of Mitrofan's jacket is a point of dispute, Prostakova consistently berates and belittles her timid husband. A short time later Mitrofan enters to comment upon a bad dream he had just had in which he saw his mother beating his father: he sympathized with his mother since such belaboring was an exhausting task (I, 110). Prostakova defends her treatment of her husband on the grounds of his remarkable stupidity. "Sometimes he just falls into a trance, as we say around here," she comments to Milon. "Sometimes he'll stand in one place for a solid hour with his eyes bugging out. . . . And then when the trance passes, uncle, he'll start talking such rubbish, uncle, that you'd ask the Lord to send a trance down on him again" (I, 123–24). Prostakov is probably not so much stupid as terrorized by his wife, for some of his asides indicate that he understands what is transpiring rather well. But he also knows what his wife demands of him, and for the sake of domestic peace he resolves to comply with those demands.

III *The Positive Characters*

By any purely statistical reading of *The Minor*, the positive characters occupy at least as important a place in the action as the negative ones. They are much more abstract and less individualized, however, and their language is smoothly literary, not nearly so rich in local dialect and slang. If a quotation from one of them has entered the language, it is entirely on a literary level, and not as a popular saying or proverb of sorts. In the twentieth century the positive characters tend to be either overlooked or explained away.

Such was not the situation in Fonvizin's day. In the "Letter to Starodum," the first piece designed for publication in the periodical Fonvizin hoped to issue in 1788, Fonvizin says that he "owes the success of his comedy *The Minor* to your person," and declares that the theater-going public even now listens to Starodum's extensive dialogues with Milon, Pravdin, and Sofya "with pleasure" (II, 40). That the positive characters should have been to such a degree responsible for the play's popularity is difficult for us to understand now. Perhaps the situation derived from the desire of the general public to hear the existing regime criticized on the stage, which would explain the censor's delaying its staging in Fonvizin's native Moscow. But the positive characters are the chief articulators of the author's positive prescriptions for society, just as the Prostakov family bears his negative critique of society. Fonvizin's constructive proposals for society's reformation moved on two levels: the (positive) internal conversion of the individual spirit to the good, and the (negative) power of the state to prevent abuses of individual power through direct intervention. The positive characters exhibit very little humor, if we except an occasional note of sarcasm directed at some folly committed by the Prostakovs. They are entirely serious in demeanor and speech, and that emphasizes the dichotomy within the play, since the humor and light entertainment are supplied by the negative characters.

As a result of this division, as Marvin Kantor has pointed out, Starodum does not seek to combat Prostakova with argumentation, since "the refutation might be lost in the buffoonery of such a dramatic confrontation."[22] There simply is, and can be, no mutual meeting of minds between the two groups of characters. The audience receives thorough guidance as to which it should prefer, but in the end the dispute between the philosophies of the two groups is resolved by the exercise of power.

Occasionally a critic writing on Fonvizin has sought to grapple with the problem of the play's positive characters. Prominent among them was Grigory Gukovsky, who in an interesting though not entirely persuasive article of 1946 formulated a rationale for approaching

these characters in a new spirit.[23] Gukovsky urged theatrical produc-
ers and directors to look upon the positive characters not as pale
abstractions, but as "live people," engaged in a fierce struggle both to
determine Sofya's personal fate and to attain ultimate influence
within the social order. Starodum, Gukovsky holds, is a "powerful
individual" who speaks sharply, quickly, energetically, constantly
interrupting his interlocutor; he is an "impulsive, heated man."
Sofya, he argues, is a "pure and healthy image, full of feminine
passion," and Milon is an "enthusiast," an eighteenth-century
forerunner of Alexander Griboedov's great creation Chatsky (*Woe
from Wit*). In early performances of *The Minor*, Gukovsky believes,
these characters were presented vigorously, not as goody-goodies;
only if the play is interpreted in this way can the plot's full drama be
evoked.

If there did exist a tradition of playing Starodum and his allies as
vigorous characters, it had surely faded by the time Vyazemsky wrote
his study of Fonvizin, for he suggests that Starodum's role should be
divided into two facets: the active participant in the play's plot, and
the *raisonneur*, or exponent of moral values, "something like the
chorus in an ancient tragedy." In this latter capacity, Vyazemsky
decreed, Starodum was incurably boring.[24] As we have seen, audiences of the 1780s did not feel quite this way: Starodum appealed to
them most in his function as *raisonneur*. As David Welsh writes in his
study of the Russian comedy, his speeches comprise nearly 20
percent of the play's total dialogue,[25] and Fonvizin must have
believed himself justified in devoting so much attention in the play to
Starodum's views.

Starodum dominates both the action and the moral atmosphere of
the play. The ground is prepared for his appearance in the first act,
when his letter arrives and casts the Prostakov household into
confusion: Prostakova at first refuses to believe he could still be alive,
since she has been praying for his soul for several years (I, 113).
Before long, however, she must accept the incontrovertible evidence
of his continued existence. Further information about him is provided in the second act, for example by Pravdin, who knows him both
personally and by reputation. "What some people call gloominess and
coarseness in him," he remarks to Sofya, "is simply his directness.
His tongue has never said 'yes' when his soul felt 'no' " (I, 124).
Starodum actually appears at the Prostakov estate only at the
beginning of Act Three.

Starodum bears one of the most outstanding "speaking names" in eighteenth-century Russian literature. Composed of the words for "old" and "thought," it points to the man's adherence to the tested, traditional verities. His experience of life, controlled by his ethical sense, has enabled him to formulate a number of generalized "rules" of morality, which he is ever ready to present for the edification of others. Immediately upon arriving he begins to talk about his background, and says he regards "rank" as something of no importance. Although he could not have been born earlier than toward the end of Peter's reign, he was educated by his father, who had been a military man at the Court of Peter the Great. Courtiers of that period, he says, were trained in military discipline and integrity, and a proper education set Starodum himself upon the right path (I, 129).

Starodum does not adhere to customs and traditions solely because they are old. Fonvizin makes this clear in a passage in which Mrs. Prostakova—who is also, after all, of Starodum's generation—remarks that she too was brought up in the old ways, when learning was at a total discount. Her father, she recalls, used to say, "May he be no Skotinin who ever wants to learn anything" (I, 140). She proudly contrasts her son's situation with her own. Apparently the older Prostakov generation is illiterate, since no one wishes to read Starodum's letter aloud when it arrives: that task is left for Pravdin, as Mrs. Prostakova waxes indignant that girls in the contemporary age are capable of receiving and reading letters (I, 113): things were not so in her day. Thus the contrast between the two groups of characters in *The Minor* is defined not by generations, for there are positive and negative characters in both generations, but by ethical criteria. Moral virtue is the gauge by which all is to be measured, whether new or old. The lack of such virtue is all too apparent in the Prostakov family.

In Starodum's view, the important facet of upbringing is not the training of the intellect, but the inculcation of moral values. Ideally, one should be trained both intellectually and morally, but if one must choose, it is better to be virtuous and ignorant than intellectually brilliant and morally vicious. As it happens, Fonvizin usually endows his morally virtuous characters with both intelligence and this world's goods.

The entire problem of virtue, and that of social justice, is central to *The Minor*. It is important to realize, however, that the struggle between the forces of evil and those of virtue is not an equal one, but that the latter are superior all along. After the Prostakov environment has been sketched in all its ghastliness in the first act, we learn from a conversation between Pravdin and Milon at the very beginning of the second that the Prostakov tyranny is almost certainly doomed. Pravdin tells Milon that he has been assigned the responsibility of investigating local estates for the purpose of taking action against landowners who mistreat their serfs. The governor of the province, he says, thinks of nothing but aiding "suffering humanity," so that the "safety of the inhabitants" under his authority is assured (I, 117). Pravdin has already spent three days with the Prostakovs, interpreted the situation correctly, and prepared the ground for action. "I hope," he says, "soon to put an end to the wife's malice and the husband's stupidity. I have already informed our chief about all the barbaric things being done here, and I have no doubt measures will be taken to eliminate them" (I, 118).

The fact that the Prostakovs will be punished for their misdeeds is thus made clear to the spectator—though not to the Prostakovs—as soon as this can reasonably be done. The spectator knows that the Prostakovs are in effect dancing along a precipice. They believe they possess the power to treat their serfs as they wish, but in fact they do not: they are ultimately powerless. When Pravdin confronts Mrs. Prostakova in the final act, she falls back upon the legal freedoms of the gentry, referring to the legislation of 1762 which buttressed the rights of the nobility over their serfs. But Pravdin responds firmly that "no one is free to tyrannize over others," and thereupon announces that her estates have been taken into trusteeship, for she has proven an "inhumane master, whose vices cannot be tolerated in a well-ordered state" (I, 172). Once this action is taken, Prostakova has no recourse in the law. The state at the highest level possesses absolute power which it exercises to enforce the rule of virtue. Consequently, there can be no question of virtue's eventual triumph. The play's interest lies largely in watching the Prostakovs wind the rope ever more ingeniously around their own necks.

The power of the state to enforce the requirements of virtue, incidentally, was not something Fonvizin concocted out of thin air, for the Russian autocracy did indeed intervene on certain occasions to end abuses of power by individual landowners. An instance of this with which Fonvizin must have been familiar involved Fedor Dmitriev-Mamonov (1727–1805), a relative of his on his mother's side and a very minor literary figure. In 1778 the Sovereign began to receive reports that he was tyrannizing over his serfs, and consequently in March of 1779 she ordered that his estates be taken into trusteeship.[26] This provided an obvious precedent for Pravdin's action.

At one point Starodum suggests that it is within the power of the state so to structure itself and society as to reward virtue in a material sense, and thus make it self-enforcing, in an instructive anticipation of a scheme set forth in 1863 by the radical critic Nikolay Chernyshevsky in his novel *What Is to Be Done?* Chernyshevsky thought society could eventually be arranged in such a way that it would be in people's self-interest to adhere to the good. So also in *The Minor*, after delivering a tirade against flatterers, Starodum responds to Pravdin's query as to how people can be made good:

> That is within the power of the Tsar. As soon as people realize that they cannot make a career without virtue; that it is impossible either through flattery or money to acquire that which is given only for merit; that individuals are selected for positions, and positions not purloined by individuals—then everyone will find it to his advantage to be virtuous, and everyone will become good (I, 168).

The only problem is how to restructure society so that it is to everyone's material advantage to be virtuous—in a word, to establish a state which functions as if it were itself virtuous—and all the individuals within it will become virtuous. The answer obviously is complex, but Fonvizin clearly implied that at the highest levels some progress toward it had been made. Not only does Pravdin resolve the situation in *The Minor* through the authority of the government; in *The Brigadier* as well Dobrolyubov wins his court case by bypassing the lower courts and bringing his complaint to the attention of the highest authorities, who then issue "strict instructions" in his favor (I, 81). As we have already noted, the Sofyas of both plays end up materially well rewarded for their virtue, the earlier one because her fiancé wins his lawsuit, the later one because she inherits her uncle's income. In a small way the positive characters at the end of *The Minor* illustrate how a social order should function in order to reward virtue. Mitrofan's two outside instructors are dismissed at the play's conclusion. Kuteykin presents an outrageous bill for his services, a bill in which he has included everything he can think of—and under ordinary circumstances, no doubt, he would receive most or all of what he requested. Tsyfirkin, however, seeks nothing, on the ground that his charge has learned nothing. Kuteykin is thoroughly put to shame and obtains no compensation at all, whereas Milon, Starodum, and Pravdin all voluntarily grant Tsyfirkin sums of money "because of his good heart" (I, 174–76). In the ideal society, we understand, honesty and goodness would be materially rewarded in some such manner, while avarice and effrontery would gain nothing.

Finally, an important subtheme in *The Minor* is that of the education of the young. In Mitrofan's case this is little better than a farce. As was the custom with young men of his social class, he is educated at home by a tutor, Vralman, who scarcely knows any more than his charge. Worse than that, he makes common cause with Mrs. Prostakova in sheltering him from such education as his other two teachers, Kuteykin and Tsyfirkin, seek to impart to him. Vralman argues that formal education is of no use to a member of the nobility, and thus undermines the efforts of his two colleagues.

The three tutors are utilized principally for comic effect, especially in such slapstick scenes as the final scene of Act Three, in which the two outside teachers almost give Vralman a drubbing. But in addition the two scenes in which Mitrofan is examined are entirely farcical. In the first such scene (scene seven of Act Three) Mitrofan is preparing for the outside examiners. When Tsyfirkin asks him to divide 300 rubles among three people, Mrs. Prostakova interrupts to object that under the conditions of the problem he should never agree to share the money at all. When Mitrofan is asked to add 10 and 10 and has difficulty in adding 1 and 1, his mother excuses and defends him, as does Vralman.

The important examination is conducted by Pravdin and Starodum, in scene eight of Act Four. Mitrofan turns out to have only the most distorted notion of grammar, and his mother comes to his defense by arguing that a nobleman has no need of learning: it is quite feasible to extort money from your subordinates and exploit your serfs without the slightest knowledge of grammar. As for history, Mitrofan knows even less of that, and when he is asked about geography he breaks into a cold sweat, since he does not know what it is. When Starodum explains that geography is useful for knowing where one wishes to go, Mrs. Prostakova replies in a famous passage:

Why, what are coachmen for? That's their business. This is no science for the gentry. A member of the gentry just says: take me there, and he'll be taken wherever he wants. Believe me, uncle, anything Mitrofanushka doesn't know is obviously nonsense. (I, 163)

And with that we have the final word of the Prostakovs of this world on the training of the intellect: anything they do not know is not worth knowing. Learning is for the inferior classes; it is unworthy of the attention of a member of the nobility.

The intertwined themes of true nobility and education are central to the unfinished short comedy on which Fonvizin was evidently working at his death, *The Selection of a Tutor.* In this play Prince Slaboumov (Weakminded) and his wife, members of the highest hereditary nobility, seeking a tutor for their spoiled son, must choose between an honest Russian, Nelstetsov, and a Frenchman, Pelikanov, whose chief academic qualifications are his skill at pulling teeth and removing corns and his eagerness to address his employers as *votre altesse.* During his interview with the prince and his wife, Nelstetsov declares his intention of educating their son as a nobleman should be educated, without any particular allowance for his noble birth. Nelstetsov will seek to inculcate in his pupil the moral virtues, showing him that "since he is of noble birth, he should have a noble soul as well" (I, 195–96). On the intellectual level, he plans to instruct the boy first in the fundamentals of the Russian Orthodox faith, then in Latin (I, 198).

When Pelikanov arrives, he turns out to be an undesirable individual who has already been driven from another district of the country for having "corrupted the hearts and heads of young noblemen." Like Vralman, he is exposed for what he truly is, and put to shame.

Although the plot is not fully resolved, at the play's end it appears that the prince and his emptyheaded wife will decline to engage Nelstetsov as a tutor, since they are guided in their actions by "ignorant pride," and an entirely false concept of the meaning of nobility.

Education was of great importance to Russian culture, as Fonvizin saw it, but virtue was even more so. Thus *The Minor* is at bottom about a conflict between moral virtue and moral vice, embodied in two groups of characters. Since that conflict is a serious one, its resolution—the revocation of Mrs. Prostakova's authority—can evoke no more than bitter laughter. The training of the intellect is secondary to this, and may be treated humorously, even as farce, for all that it is likewise a social good. As Starodum remarks, "the chief purpose of all human knowledge" must be virtue (I, 168). If Fonvizin sought, in the Neoclassical manner, to combine the pleasant with the useful, to instruct while amusing, then he attempted to guide his contemporaries along the paths of moral and social virtue. That was the political significance of his play. In the course of attaining his objective, however, he created a literary work which helped mold the image which Russians held of themselves and whose personages have since assumed a life of their own in a fashion characteristic of classic works of a national literature.

CHAPTER 5

Russia and Europe: The Travel Letters

I Communicating from Abroad

THE works usually referred to as the *Travel Letters* are those
which Fonvizin composed during his journey to Germany and
France in 1777–78 and his visit in Germany and Italy in 1784–85.[1]
The letters from the first journey are approximately evenly divided
between those addressed to his family in Moscow and those sent to
Count Peter Panin, also in Moscow. The letters from the second
journey consist almost entirely of missives to his family, with only two
surviving letters addressed to Peter Panin. The letters to his relatives
are more chattily intimate, the epistles to Panin more formal.

The content of the travel letters is understandably heterogeneous.
Fonvizin writes about nearly everything which might have some
relevance to the travels upon which he is embarked. These include
comments on the vicissitudes of travel at that time; remarks on his
own health and that of his wife (the first journey was undertaken
largely for the purpose of curing her of a tapeworm, a process which
Fonvizin summarizes with some care); descriptions of the cities and
architectural monuments which they have visited (although he has
little to say of the natural beauties of the countryside); accounts of
meetings with local dignitaries; observations on the local population;
generalizations about the national characters of the people they were
visiting; comparisons of foreign cultures with Russian culture; and so
forth. Cast in an easy colloquial style, they set off to advantage the
mind of an intelligent and interested eighteenth-century Russian
who undertook an unmediated investigation of contemporary Western European culture. Fonvizin's reactions to what he sees are very
personal, and his letters represent a break with the impersonal
Neoclassical tradition: they paint a portrait of a strong personality
unafraid to picture himself as he is. Even now the travel letters
remain very much worth reading as a chronicle of the contact

between a remarkable Russian and European civilization of the eighteenth century.

It is not wholly clear that Fonvizin designed his letters for general circulation originally, although he evidently intended to include some of them in his *Collected Works* of 1788. In the back of his mind at the time he may have considered printing the letters he sent to Panin. Pigarev assumes that Fonvizin intended these missives as a "unique sort of literary work in epistolary form,"[2] and N.S. Tikhonravov has dubbed them a "satirical journey," to distinguish them from the "sentimental" journeys of a Lawrence Sterne or a Nikolay Karamzin.[3] Certainly Fonvizin's letters do not share the Sentimentalist and allegorical elements of Nikolay Radishchev's *Journey from St. Petersburg to Moscow* (published in 1790), a summons to radical social reform lacking many points of contact with the Russian reality from which it sprang. Karamzin's *Letters of a Russian Traveler* (published during the 1790s) cover some of the same geographical territory as Fonvizin's, but the author views Western Europe through rose-colored, Sentimentalist glasses, and can hardly bring himself to say anything unfavorable about the people or places he encounters. Much of Karamzin's time was devoted to visiting great figures of literature and scholarship, such as Immanuel Kant, in whom he discerned only good. Although he never ceases to be a Russian, neither does the gentle Karamzin display any wish to set himself apart especially from those whom he met.

Fonvizin's approach could scarcely have been more different. His mocking eye detects the weaknesses and illogicalities in all with which he comes in contact; he sharpens conflicts instead of eliding them. The eminent nineteenth-century critic Apollon Grigorev put it well when he remarked that the reader of Fonvizin's travel letters is most impressed by the "appropriateness and malicious justice of his comments."[4] For Fonvizin was a satirist, and his tended to be a jaundiced eye. It was so jaundiced, in fact, as to repel some of his biographers. Leone Savoj has denounced his travel writings as chauvinistic,[5] and Fonvizin's first biographer, Petr Vyazemsky, criticized him severely. As an adept of things French, Vyazemsky was particularly incensed by Fonvizin's critical attitude toward that nation, and decided that Fonvizin had not really been the sort to benefit from foreign travel: "A Russian born and bred," the critic wrote, "when abroad he was somehow constrained and out of place." And what Grigorev interpreted as the "malicious justice" of his general approach, Vyazemsky saw as something quite different:

"Fonvizin's malice [*zloslovie*] is cold and dry: it reeks of the preaching of the overinflated orator, convinces no one, and simply causes us to regret that even a brilliant mind can suffer its eclipses."[6]

In order to bolster his case against the object of his researches, Vyazemsky showed that Fonvizin had borrowed several passages in his letters from a book of 1751 by C. P. Duclos, well-known in the France of that time, entitled *Considérations sur les moeurs de ce siècle*. Duclos was a keen observer of the French national character, an unsystematic sociologist with a gift for the accurate and epigrammatic generalization, and Fonvizin no doubt found him intellectually congenial. Vyazemsky, however, accused Fonvizin not only of something bordering on plagiarism, but even of intellectual dishonesty in pirating principally passages in which Duclos had negative things to say of his countrymen, while ignoring his positive evaluations of them.[7] Recently Alexis Strycek has demonstrated that Fonvizin borrowed more extensively from Duclos than Vyazemsky knew, but he also points out that all the borrowings occur at the beginning of one particular letter,[8] and also are taken from early chapters of Duclos's book. The letter in question, written from Aachen in September of 1778 to Panin, begins with a lengthy and rather formal disquisition on the French national character. Fonvizin must have been reading Duclos at the time and, finding his pithy formulations informative and entertaining, wove them into the fabric of his essay. There may have been a certain element of intellectual dishonesty in this exercise, but Fonvizin was not writing a scholarly treatise, and he delimited his borrowings strictly. Even if it could be shown that many of the memorable formulations scattered through his letters had been purloined, this would only slightly reduce the general interest they hold for today's reader. Strycek also shows that Fonvizin's account of his visit to the French Academy owes much to a newspaper report of the same event; and that Fonvizin took portions of his Italian letters from the description of an Italian journey published in German in 1781.[9] It is almost certain that further investigation would show Fonvizin borrowed from still other contemporary sources, much as Karamzin borrowed and paraphrased widely in his *Letters of a Russian Traveler*.[10] Travel letters were among the most eclectic of genres; one could make observations on the most varied subjects in them, and incorporate the most varied materials into them. It is not too astonishing that, in doing so, Fonvizin sometimes crossed the line of what we would now consider permissible. But, despite Vyazemsky, this gives us no license to denigrate the value of his travel letters.

II *France and Russia*

France was the country whose culture most exercised Fonvizin's imagination. This was quite understandable, since France enjoyed cultural supremacy in the Europe of that day, and especially over Russia, where the aristocracy frequently spoke French as its first language. As a Russian "born and bred," in Vyazemsky's phrase, Fonvizin wished to examine French culture on its home grounds. The authority he gained from a visit to France would, he hoped, enable him to bring intelligent Russians to a more critical appreciation of French culture.

Fonvizin believed that his countrymen suffered from a distorted view of France, as he had demonstrated by his attack on Gallomania in *The Brigadier*. Nothing was worse, he thought, than blind and unquestioning allegiance to a foreign culture over one's own. In his travel letters he argued that every culture has its strengths and weaknesses, and that Russian culture could hold its own by comparison with Western European cultures.

Fonvizin probably felt a certain moral obligation to be loyal to his national culture. As David Welsh points out in his study of eighteenth-century Russian comedy, Fonvizin's old associate Vladimir Lukin had argued that there was a definite linkage between admiration for a foreign culture and susceptibility to immoral influences,[11] and Fonvizin probably tended to agree with him on this point. A Russian Gallomane was despicable enough if he stayed in Russia, Fonvizin thought, but he would encounter sure ruin if he visited France itself before he was morally and spiritually prepared. Thus in a letter of 1778 Fonvizin remarks that a father should never permit his son to visit Paris until he is at least twenty-five years of age. The city, he said, resembled the "plague," one which damaged its victims more morally than physically: it was capable of transforming a young man who otherwise might have developed into an honest citizen into a "giddypate incapable of doing anything" (II, 477). During their sojourn in Paris the Fonvizins had met most of the Russian colony, and the writer made this prognosis on the basis of observation. Most of the Russian Parisians, he said, made "day out of night and night out of day," abandoning themselves to the pleasures of gaming and sexual adventure. He knew of only two Russians who had escaped this Parisian "plague," and who were therefore, slightingly, termed "philosophers," which undoubtedly meant merely that they rejected the dissipated way of life of their deracinated compatriots (II, 439).

On the other hand, Fonvizin also thought that the poison of Gallic culture could, in appropriate dosages, have a tonic effect upon the young, at least upon those who were fundamentally morally stable. At least he so argues in an often-quoted prescription for dealing with the young who exhibit signs of estrangement from their native land:

> If any of my youthful countrymen who have solid good sense should become indignant over the abuses and confusions prevalent in Russia and in his heart begin to feel alienated from her, then there is no better method of converting him to the love he should feel for his Fatherland than to send him to France as quickly as possible. Here he will quickly discover that all the tales about the perfection of everything here are absolutely false. . . . (II, 467)

If we wonder how the same treatment may produce such divergent effects on different individuals, the key to this prescription must surely be the requirement that the young man possess "good sense." Most of the Frenchified Russians then resident in Paris lacked this entirely. They were there for the wrong reasons, and devoted their time to the frivolous life.

Fonvizin visited France, not in order to associate with other Russians, but to learn how the French actually lived in their own land. To be sure, he entered upon this task with some anti-French inclinations. Thus, in his first letter from Montpellier in 1777, he describes his departure from Germany and his arrival in his first French city, Landau: "When we rode into the city we were assaulted by a horrid stench, which left us in no doubt that we had entered France" (II, 418). That stench—both physical and moral—never left the Fonvizins' nostrils entirely during their visit.

Fonvizin took a lively interest in the standard French tourist attractions, including architecture and also local ceremonies, both political and religious. He was willing to give credit where he thought it due, as when he commented on the excellence of French roads (II, 418). But he was most concerned with analyzing the character of the French people, those approaches and attitudes typical of the leading culture of his day.

As a visitor Fonvizin was a firsthand observer of French hospitality:

how well they fed themselves, how well they entertained their guests. He found the economies which the French practiced absolutely astonishing. Once, he reported, when out for a walk in Montpellier he dropped in unexpectedly at the home of a certain Marquise who was among the city's wealthiest women, only to discover her dining in the kitchen with the servants in order to spare the expense of kindling a fire in the dining room, since they had no guests (II, 431–32). Although Fonvizin realized that firewood was relatively expensive in France, he did not believe that cost justified such unusual procedures. And then even when the French had guests, they tended to be unacceptably tight-fisted: they did not pass dishes around the table lest the guests take too much, or leave bottles of wine on the table, since the guests were then tempted to drink excessively. Fonvizin's vision was so poor he could not see what to request from the other end of the table, and thus he ordinarily "got up from the table hungry" (II, 431). Fonvizin acknowledged the excellence of French cuisine, but French hospitality could not stand comparison with the Russian. Then too, he was astonished to discover that the table linen in the best French homes was filthy, much worse than that to be found even in rather impoverished Russian residences. When he inquired as to the reason for this, he was informed that, since one did not eat napkins and tablecloths, there was no need for them to be clean, an "absurd conclusion," in Fonvizin's words (II, 429).

Observation convinced Fonvizin that the French were extraordinarily self-centered, both individually and collectively. "Friendship, family, honesty, gratitude"—all these things had no meaning for them, he decided. They ignored the deeper virtues, and attended only to what lay on the surface. "External appearance substitutes for everything else here," he wrote. "Be polite, that is don't contradict anybody in anything; and be pleasant, that is, rattle off anything that comes into your head: these are the two rules you must follow in order to be *un homme charmant*" (II, 444). Everywhere in France Fonvizin perceived only spiritual emptiness and the lack of any true social concern. Allied to this personal self-centeredness was a cultural self-centeredness, which expressed itself in total disinterest in any foreign cultures. Despite the high level of French culture and the easy availability of information, Fonvizin observed that "many people hear [from us] for the first time that there is such a place as Russia in the world and that we Russians speak a different language than they do" (II, 423). Even the pro-French Karamzin later found the French just as ignorant of things Russian, although he did not become so upset about it as did Fonvizin.

Fonvizin also discovered that French ignorance extended to many areas other than geography. He found the French sadly lacking in intellectual curiosity and in factual information. And the common people, he said, were ignorant idlers ready to believe any faker with a sense of style: "On every street you can find a group of people surrounding some charlatan who is pulling tricks, selling wondrous medicines, and entertaining the idiots with jokes" (II, 428). In short, Fonvizin declared, the common people in France were "lazy" and "very coarse" (II, 429). "I think," he wrote at another point, "that there is not a nation in the world which is more credulous and has less common sense" (II, 433).

Unlike the lower classes, the French upper classes were at least capable of camouflaging their intellectual emptiness with a certain flair. Unfortunately, a little further probing laid bare the superficiality of the French mind. The French esteem wit *(ostrota)*, he decided, more highly than sense *(razum)*, and therefore were not truly concerned with truth (II, 472–73). Everyone has an opinion which he articulates with impressive confidence, but ordinarily this is merely the opinion of the person to whom the Frenchman is speaking, and with whom he considers it bad form to disagree (II, 473). Fonvizin experimented amusingly with this trait of the French mind. For instance, when the subject of freedom came up, he recalled,

I would begin my remarks by saying that, as far as I could tell, this basic human right was religiously observed in France; whereupon I would ecstatically be told *que le Francais est né libre*, that this right is their genuine good fortune and that they would die rather than permit it to be infringed upon in the slightest. After listening to this, I would start to talk about various inconveniences I had encountered and would little by little expound the notion that it would be a good thing if freedom were something more than a mere empty phrase. And then those same people . . . would immediately say to me: *O monsieur, vous avez raison! Le Francais est écrasé, le Francais est esclave.* And they would thereupon fall into an absolute ecstasy of denunciation. . . . (II, 463)

Fonvizin considered this intellectual instability a judgment on French culture: it showed that the French simply skimmed along the surface of things, and lacked any deep convictions. This trait also emerged, he thought, in the French love of swindling and deception, which depend upon verbal facility. "They consider deception the right of intellect," he wrote (II, 481): deception was a species of intellectual competition in which the shrewdest and most unprincipled contestant won. Like most other people, the French deceive for the sake of money, but they would not resort to genuinely foul crimes. They will murder only if they are starving, he thought: "Once a Frenchman has enough to eat he won't murder anyone, but will be satisfied with swindling others" (II, 481).

Unlike Karamzin, who admired most of the great intellectual figures whom he met during his journeys, Fonvizin adopted a bilious view even of the greatest French writers and intellectuals, those with worldwide reputations. Fonvizin claimed to have encountered virtually all the leading French intellectuals except Rousseau. Many of the well-known French philosophers visited the Fonvizin residence, he reported, and thus he had the opportunity to observe them carefully. Upon reflection, he found them almost all "worthy of contempt." Their chief traits of character were "arrogance, envy, and deception"; they spent their time denigrating others and lauding themselves (II, 443–44). Fonvizin could hardly discover words sufficiently strong to express his distaste for French intellectuals he had encountered. Almost the only dispensation he granted from this blanket condemnation was to Antoine-Leonard Thomas, author of the "Eulogy of Marcus Aurelius," which he had himself translated. Fonvizin thought Thomas's "humility and honesty" appealing, while his fellows displayed only "arrogance, falsehood, love of gain, and despicable flattery." Philosophers, he concluded, appear to derive little personal benefit from their philosophy (II, 476).

The immorality which the French exhibited in the intellectual sphere was even more rampant in the area of sexual mores. At one point Fonvizin composed a small essay on Parisian mistresses, or prostitutes. At the theater and at home, he said, immoral women were covered with diamonds and enjoyed all the perquisites of wealth, to the point where honest women sought to wear as little jewelry as possible. When society went driving on holidays, all the finest carriages were occupied by prostitutes. Paris was a city in which the immoral prospered, while people of any principle starved. The entire place was simply a sink of iniquity, a Sodom and Gomorrah (II, 446).

On the whole, Fonvizin took a rather dim view of France and things French. A leitmotif of disillusion—perhaps not wholly sincere—runs through the travel letters. "I was never so mistaken in my life," he wrote from Paris in March of 1778, "as in my ideas about France" (II, 441). The propaganda of the Russian Gallomanes on behalf of the "earthly paradise" had affected even Fonvizin's thinking. Now that he had walked the streets of that "paradise," he could evaluate it realistically. Indeed, Fonvizin perhaps overdid his criticism of France as a means of correcting the distorted Russian perception of France: exaggerated propaganda required an exagerated critique as a counter.

A characteristic of France which both Fonvizin and Karamzin noted was the coexistence, cheek by jowl, of the bad with the good, the foul with the pure. Paris provided the greatest example of this: "at every step when I find something quite excellent, there will always be something right next to it which is bad and barbaric" (II, 439). There were facets of French life which deserved praise, and Fonvizin wrote of them, although he was always prepared to terminate that exposition in order to comment on something "bad and barbaric." He considered many of the French provincial cities scarcely worth seeing even once, but the capital was another matter. Paris was an "entire world"; with its size and population it occupied a unique place among cities (II, 438). The playwright was entranced by the cultural riches which the city offered to visitor and native alike.

Prominent among those cultural riches was the theater, which Fonvizin was quick to visit. His general impression was that French comedy had attained the highest possible level, while tragedy was more inferior than he had anticipated (II, 440). A short time later he returned to the subject of the theater, saying that "anyone who has not seen comedy in Paris has no idea of what comedy is" (II, 445–46). The actors formed such a perfect ensemble and interacted so ideally that a person who had once seen French comedy could never be satisfied with anything else. But then French music subsisted on an incredibly low level. He had never heard such "goats" of singers before, and his wife kept cotton with her to stuff in her ears as soon as a French chorus broke into song (II, 425).

The French as a people also had some positive traits. Fonvizin particularly approved of their devotion to their country and the Crown. The lowliest chimney-sweep, he said, was "ecstatic if he should happen to see his king"; the French were totally devoted to their Fatherland, and would not abandon it under any circumstances. The finest thing in which the French might instruct Russians, Fonvizin said, would be "love for the Fatherland and their monarch" (II, 443). These observations, incidentally, fit poorly with the claims of some Fonvizin specialists that he sensed the coming French Revolution.

Fonvizin also observed that the French valued scholarship and learning very highly, and said there was not in France "a single scholar who is not provided for" (II, 443). True, he had a low opinion of the scholars in question, but he could only praise the French for their respect for learning.

In the numerous other comments he made about the French and their culture, Fonvizin adhered to the overall view that France, like any other country, was a mixture of good and bad, but focused his attention primarily on the latter. Early in his visit to France, before he had seen Paris, he summarized his approach in a passage which will apply very well to all his foreign sojourns:

> In short, all the travelers are lying unconscionably when they describe France as an earthly paradise. Without question there are many good things here, but I'm not sure at all whether there aren't more bad things. At any rate, up to now my wife and I still believe it is infinitely better to live in St. Petersburg. (II, 420)

III   Germans, Italians, and Others

France intrigued Fonvizin more than any other foreign country, and it was the object of his journey of 1777–78. In 1784–85 his objective was Italy, which he was interested in more for its art treasures than for any other reason. Germany was merely a country through which he passed in order to arrive somewhere else. Despite his family origins, and despite the fact that German was the first modern foreign language he had studied, he wrote less about Germany than about Italy or France. Those comments on Germany he did record indicate that his attitude toward the Germans was roughly the same as his attitude toward France, or toward Italy. In 1777, for instance, on his way to Montpellier, he stopped for a time in Leipzig, a city he found well supplied with "scholars." To him, however, they seemed more like pedants: some were puffed up with pride solely because they could converse in Latin, others spent their time in abstract philosophizing lacking any connection with the realities of this world, and all this to the point where "Leipzig proves without any question that scholarship does not engender intellect" (II, 454).

During his visit of 1784, Fonvizin was out of sorts. Whereas he had complained of France's filthiness, now he carped at the astonishing cleanliness of German cities: "all the streets and houses here," he said, "are so clean that it seems like an affectation" (II, 511). In late August of 1784 the Fonvizins arrived in Nürnberg, chronicling their adventures in a journal which they described as a record of their "voluntary suffering." From Leipzig to Nürnberg, they claimed, they had wrestled with "hellish roads, dreadful food, and beds infested with bedbugs and fleas." "Here," they concluded, "everything is generally worse than in our country: the people, horses, the land, the availability of food—in short, everything in our country is better, and we are better people than the Germans are, too" (II, 508). Quite possibly there was a substantial dose of fleeting irritation in that often-quoted passage, but it is only a stronger variant of the judgment which Fonvizin usually passed on foreign cultures.

He might have said much the same thing of the Italians. When, on their way to Italy in 1784, the Fonvizins stopped in Bozen (present-day Bolzano), they experienced a foretaste of the Italian way of life: "Dirty stone floors; filthy linen; bread that beggars wouldn't eat in Russia; and clean water that we would consider slops" (II, 519). In the midst of the magnificent heritage of the Italian architectural past, Fonvizin reported, they would constantly encounter the most miserable Italian beggars suffering from extreme poverty, a situation which he attributed to the weakness of government authority (II, 545). "The old men especially are almost naked, emaciated with hunger, and usually plagued by some sort of repulsive illness," he wrote (II, 523). As in France, the barbaric and dreadful existed side by side with the exquisite; their intermingling seemed almost a rule of Western European life.

The Fonvizins spent most of their time among the cultured Italian upper classes, whom they found quite as miserly as the French, and even less interesting as conversationalists. Fonvizin reported having been invited to a large dinner at the home of a wealthy banker and blushing on his behalf, since "his formal dinner was incomparably worse than what we had every day at the inn" (II, 528). Social life was unbelievably boring—in Florence, at any rate. Hardly two out of 100 were capable of carrying on an intelligent conversation, and only a few displayed enough initiative to play cards as a means of passing the time (II, 528).

If social life was less interesting in Italy than in France, the moral level of society was lower as well. "Here the wedding day is the day of the divorce," he wrote, for the notion of marital fidelity was in total disrepute throughout Italy. Social custom decrees that as soon as a woman marries she must acquire a lover, a "true knight," who will devote all his waking hours to her. Consequently, a wife ordinarily sees her husband only when it is time to retire, which can be rather a trial for married couples in love with each other. As a result, Fonvizin wrote, "there are neither fathers nor sons" in Italy (II, 531–32).

In general Fonvizin considered Italians the most boring people he had visited, boring and tightfisted. They were accomplished swindlers as well. He told one interesting anecdote on this topic. When he was in Florence, he said, and the word spread that he was purchasing paintings and art objects, he was summoned to the splendid palace of a well-known marquis, who showed him a painting supposedly by Guido Reni and available for 1,000 gold pieces (*chervonnyi*). Not being very expert on Italian painting, Fonvizin requested and received permission to have the picture appraised. His appraisers told him that it was certainly not a Guido, and was worth at most five or six gold pieces. Upon returning the painting, Fonvizin informed the marquis of the appraisers' opinion, which quite infuriated him. But then just before Fonvizin left Florence, the marquis sent word to him that, "out of friendship," he would part with the picture for ten gold pieces (II, 534)! Fonvizin thought it amazing that a nobleman would stoop to such base deception, but also found the incident in some ways typical of the Italians.

Fonvizin's view of the nationalities with which he had less to do than with the French, Italians, or Germans, was equally negative, as a rule. For instance, he found Poland—like Germany, a way-station to somewhere else—a curious and foreign land, for all that the Poles were brother Slavs. Even the Polish upper classes were in the grip of the most fantastic superstition: they were constantly seeking to exorcise possessed individuals. As in France, the Catholic clergy bound the people to such superstition: the entire country was controlled by priests and Jews, as far as Fonvizin could see (II, 414). Despite Roman Catholic influence in Poland, public morality left much to be desired. "Quite frequently," he wrote, "you will find a husband in public with two women, the one he is now living with and the one he has just divorced," since divorce was extraordinarily easy to come by in Poland (II, 416). Fonvizin found many aspects of Polish life quite strange. Polish women, for example, dressed just as they liked, wearing caps or turbans or building their hair up into an "entire tower" on their heads. He and his wife could not reconcile themselves to the sounds of the Polish language, and spent their time at the theater giggling instead of attending to the play (II, 416). During their trip of 1777–78, incidentally, they very commonly reacted by laughing at things to which they were not accustomed. On their second journey, in 1784–85, they seem to have accepted cultural differences with more aplomb.

IV *Slavophile or Westernizer?*

As the nineteenth century wore on, there arose in Russia two great currents of thought on the question of the relationship between Russia and the West. The so-called "Westernizers" argued that Russia and her culture belonged in the European context, that Russians and West Europeans shared the same essential characteristics, and that, since Russia had developed more slowly than Western Europe, she would traverse the same historical path while benefiting from the errors of those who had preceded her. The Westernizers applauded the drastic reforms of Peter the Great as both necessary and historically desirable.

The "Slavophiles," in contrast, argued that Russia had a distinct historical destiny, differing in essence from that of Western nations. Catholic Western societies were based upon force or the threat thereof, whereas Orthodox Slavic societies were founded upon love and mutual cooperation. Russia, they maintained, should isolate herself from the diseases of Western culture in order to provide an example for the world. The Slavophiles believed that Peter the Great had done violence to Russian culture by wrenching the country from its true historical moorings.

Fonvizin dealt with many of those same problems which would agitate the Westernizers and Slavophiles many years later. He treated them in detail both in his travel letters and in some of his other writings, including his "Questions" put to Catherine in 1783 (his final question on that occasion was: "In what does our national character consist?" Catherine replied: "In the rapid and quick comprehension of everything, in exemplary obedience, and in receptivity to all virtues granted man by the Creator" [II, 275]).

Fonvizin was interested in the problem of national character, both Russian and Western European, and, as the Marxist thinker Georgy Plekhanov once noted, in the question of "what should be the relationship of Russia to the West on the basis of the Petrine reforms."[12] As a satirist, he took a jaundiced view of whatever society he was examining at the moment, which means we must clarify Fonvizin's attitude toward Russia herself, especially as it was expressed in his travel letters.

We have already seen that Fonvizin ranked France, Italy, and Germany below Russia. He thought Western moral standards to be lower than those prevalent in Russia, partly because Western religious values were less profound than those of the Orthodox. Still, if Fonvizin ranked Russia above Western Europe in these regards, he nevertheless did not rate his native land very high in absolute terms. Russia still fell far short of the ideal. He expressed this most unambiguously very late in his travels, after his stroke of 1785, when his anti-Russian sentiments were at their strongest. In 1787, upon returning from the spas of Austria, the Fonvizins arrived at the gates of Kiev, where they met a young lad who offered to guide them to an inn. A thunderstorm came up just as they approached the inn, and they pounded vainly at the gates for an hour seeking admission as the rains descended. Finally the owner appeared and asked who was there. The boy, seizing the opportunity, cried "Open up: these are relatives of Prince Potemkin's!" Thereupon the doors instantly flew open and they entered the courtyard. "And here we knew," Fonvizin concluded, "that we were back in Russia" (II, 570–71). The combination is instructive: Russian laziness and unwillingness to put oneself out for travelers in distress, galvanized by a bold lie into immediate accommodation. Though Fonvizin spoke humorously as he recorded this tale, it was a serious instance of some of the more unattractive workings of the Russian mind.

The questions Fonvizin addressed to Catherine in 1783 embrace a mixture of political and social topics, if by "social" we mean points having to do with the national character. His queries imply that Russians love to quarrel about things which ought to be obvious; they contract debts without thinking; they have nothing to talk about in society; they attach no stigma to those who contribute nothing to society; they cannot write properly; and they tend to initiate projects with great enthusiasm which in short order evaporates. The question concluding the entire series ("In what does our national character consist?") may be an indication to the reader that many of the preceding questions pointed to Fonvizin's notion of the Russian character. His penultimate question, moreover, indicated his concept of the proper relationship between Russia and the West: "How might we eliminate two contradictory and equally harmful prejudices: the first, that in our country everything is bad and everything abroad is good; and the second, that abroad everything is bad and everything in our country is good?" (II, 275).

The phrasing of this question implies that the true relationship between cultures was a complex one. Neither Western Europe nor Russia enjoyed a monopoly on virtue: as he wrote in 1778, "I have seen that in any country there is much more bad than good, and that people are people everywhere" (II, 449). In the final accounting the individual is the measure of the society in which he lives. Before long Fonvizin arrived at a form of cultural internationalism, which he articulated most succinctly in a letter of September 1778 analyzing the French character in some detail. "Worthwhile people," he wrote then, "no matter to which nation they may belong, form a single nation among themselves" (II, 480). Such individuals recognize one another instantly, as Fonvizin had recognized Thomas, and should support and sustain one another. They also realize that they are in a tiny minority anywhere: as Fonvizin claimed, one could spend years in Italy without ever encountering an honest man (II, 533). Here the phrase "honest man" is equivalent to "worthwhile people," those schooled in the ways of virtue who form the "single nation" to which Fonvizin believed he belonged. An individual's happiness depended upon his inner being, and not in general upon the social milieu in which he found himself. "If anybody tries to tell you that Paris is a center of entertainment and merriment," he wrote to his relatives from the French capital in 1778, "don't believe him. . . . A person who lacks resources within himself will live the same life in Paris as in Uglich. Four walls are the same everywhere . . ."(II, 444–45).

Although he is not very consistent, Fonvizin displays a tendency to define a national character in terms of negative traits, and to subsume positive traits of national character into the composite picture of an international of virtuous people. He dwells in more detail on those aspects of the French and Italian character which seemed to him ridiculous or contemptible; and when he did discover individuals who embodied admirable national traits, he had an inclination to admit them to the "single nation" of "worthwhile people."

Fonvizin did not hold that there were no differences between national cultures and national characters, for he thought there were; but most of the differences emerged in Russia's favor, so that a good Russian was well advised to stay at home. In so holding he articulated and presaged some of the cultural arguments which would engross

Russian intellectuals several decades later. One passage from the travel letters is particularly interesting in that connection:

It really is true that intelligent people are rare everywhere. If here [in Western Europe] people began to live before us, then at least we, at the beginning of our life's path, may mold ourselves in the form we wish to, and avoid those inconveniences and evils which have taken firm root here. *Nous commençons et ils finissent.* I think that a person who has just been born is more fortunate than one who is at the point of death. (II, 493)

Aside from the more general questions of historical understanding which this passage raises, Fonvizin's formulation is an amalgam of the positions which the Slavophiles and Westernizers would adopt at a later time. Fonvizin articulates the Westernizing idea that Russia would tread the same historical path as the West, but with a chronological lag, and thus would benefit from the previous experience of the West. But concurrently Fonvizin brings in the proto-Slavophile notion of the collapse of the West, the idea that Russia is coming into the world at a point when Western societies are in some sense "dying." And if Fonvizin's loyalty to the traditions of Peter the Great links him with the Westernizers, his insistence on the overall moral—if not material—superiority of Russian culture unites him with the Slavophiles. Consequently, he cannot be claimed completely justifiably by either camp as its spiritual ancestor.

Finally, Fonvizin's internationalist spirit emerges in his travel writings through his keen interest in those arts—music, but especially painting and architecture—which establish communication between cultures even while allowing them to retain their national characteristics. During his trip to France in 1777, Fonvizin was apparently just beginning to acquire that expertise in art which he required for his commercial dealings. At that time he considered the art and architecture of France magnificent: "I am no connoisseur of painting," he wrote then, "but I have been standing for half an hour at a stretch in front of pictures in order to inspect them thoroughly" (II, 419). When he traveled to Germany and Italy in 1784–85, he had greatly improved his knowledge of art, and his reputation as an art buyer accompanied him everywhere. The gallery in Florence, he wrote, was splendid, and he had had several pictures copied for his own use (II, 529). For him, St. Peter's in Rome was the height of human cultural achievement: "Anyone who has seen it cannot be astonished by anything else in the world in the area of the arts" (II,

531). During another paean to St. Peter's, by the way, Fonvizin expressed the view that the art of antiquity was incomparably superior to the art of modern times ("What taste, what intellect they had in former centuries," he exclaimed). St. Peter's stood as an exception to this rule, but this was partially because its architect had imitated the art of the ancients in many particulars (II, 538). But even in his admiration for the arts, Fonvizin always retained his humor and sense of perspective. "We live only with paintings and statues," he wrote from Italy in 1784, "and I'm afraid I may turn into a bust myself" (II, 535).

This, then, was what Fonvizin required of his native culture and in foreign ones: taste, intellect, moral standards. He tried to approach foreign countries without preconceived notions, although he did declare he had been badly misled by propaganda in favor of France. Taste, intellect, and moral standards were qualities both of an individual and of a culture, and Fonvizin realized they were not to be found anywhere very frequently. Still, he was predisposed toward his native land culturally, and toward the past historically. Perhaps nations and cultures at their inception are more likely to adhere to lofty standards than they are later, when they have succumbed to the sins of adulthood or sunk into senility. As a young culture Russia could learn from the West, but she should do so without concluding that she was in any way inferior to it. The future belonged to Russia, Fonvizin believed. The West was exhausted morally, materially, and spiritually; it was living off the accumulated capital of its past. Russia was no ideal—a fact of which no one could have been more conscious than the author of *The Minor*—but it displayed the moral and intellectual vigor necessary to set an example for the world.

CHAPTER 6

Politics and Literature

I Monarchy and the Monarch

DENIS Fonvizin's literary career was inextricably intertwined
with politics. As we know, he served as a high government
official, first under Ivan Elagin, then under Nikita Panin; in this
capacity he dealt directly with questions of state, and especially with
problems of foreign policy. In what time remained to him after his
official duties, he wrote and translated, helping to create and nurture
modern Russian culture. It is noteworthy—though also more characteristic of Russian literature in the eighteenth century than in later
periods—that nearly everything he wrote or translated was of
political or social significance. The time had not yet arrived when
authors could occupy the reading public with the intricacies of
individual psychology. Instead, writers sought to assist their society
in improving itself; often enough they regarded themselves as
counselors to monarchs. Certainly Fonvizin seemed to believe that
he could affect the course of official policy through his writing, in
addition to influencing social *mores* directly and bypassing the
uncertainties of legislation.

The predominant political fact of Russian society of the eighteenth
century was the existence of the monarchy. Any writer on political
topics almost inevitably had to adopt an attitude toward both the
institution of the monarchy in general and toward the persons of
particular monarchs. If he wished to be immediately influential, he
would have to accept the basic premises of monarchical government,
even though somewhat modified. He could not simply negate the
monarchic system.

A writer was also fortunate to have powerful allies who thought as
he did. Fonvizin eventually established ties with the "party" of Count
Nikita Panin, and after its fall from power became its chief public
spokesman and ideologist in the 1780s. It is in this context that a study

103

of literature and politics in Fonvizin's writings of the 1780s particularly is of greatest interest.

In his book *The Politics of Catherinian Russia*, David Ransel argues
persuasively that the monarch even in the Russian autocracy had to
rely on one or another of the Court parties in order to rule, and for
assistance in formulating the details of particular policies. At least
since the death of Peter the Great there had been a struggle between
the Russian monarch and the highest aristocracy over the division of
supreme power. Superficially it might appear that the introduction of
some ruling aristocratic body which shared authority in a defined
manner with the monarch would be a step toward democratization of
the regime. However, in practice most of the "progressive" elements
in Russian society favored the concentration of power in the autocrat's
hands, on the grounds that the high aristocracy tended to be
politically conservative. Such, for example, had been the reaction of
Peter's theological and political theoretician Feofan Prokopovich to
attempts by the old-line aristocratic families to limit the power of the
monarchy after Peter's death; 130 years later, after the emancipation
of the serfs in 1861 effected by the centralized power of the autocracy
against the opposition of the nobility, such a renowned liberal as Ivan
Turgenev could admit that he was a "closet monarchist," because he
believed that genuine social reform would flow only from the
monarch, and not from the nobility in general. During the nineteenth
century the peasantry thought that the Tsar wanted only the good,
but that his intentions were thwarted by his subordinates.

Generally speaking, the Panin party also adhered to this point of
view; that is, it held that the monarch himself should be the source of
political and social enlightenment. Ransel notes that, during his
mission in Sweden from 1748 to 1760, Panin worked to buttress the
authority of the Swedish monarchy, which he felt had been excessively weakened.[1] In addition, the Panin party subscribed to the
ideals of the Petrine reforms, which presupposed a vital monarchy;[2]
and Fonvizin made his Starodum a staunch adherent of Petrine
traditions.

On the other hand, Fonvizin and his allies did not believe that the
power of the ruler should be boundless, for the unlimited autocrat
would almost inevitably become a despot who would not flinch at
torturing and destroying his own people to quench his lust for power.
The serious question was, not *whether* autocratic power should be
limited, but rather to what degree and in what fashion it should be
circumscribed.

One might, for instance, bound the autocratic power through formal mechanisms (the fact that, as Ransel shows, even Catherine's power was naturally limited through her dependence on Court factions was not explicitly recognized at the time). Soon after Catherine ascended the throne, Panin presented a reform project which would have introduced a permanent Imperial Council to share authority with the monarch in all legislative matters, and to coordinate the functioning of the bureaucracy as well. According to this proposal, a law could not be promulgated without the signature both of the monarch and the state secretary—the high bureaucratic official—responsible for its formulation and administration. Moreover, once the Imperial Council had been established, its members could not be removed by the Crown, though they were accountable to "the most purely aristocratic body in the Russian Empire, the Governing Senate," in Ransel's phrase. Thus, Ransel goes on, "if Panin was hoping to plant the seeds of constitutional order with his project, his ambition at this time extended no farther than to a narrowly aristocratic variety of constitutionalism."[3]

Catherine refused to accede to this severe limitation on her monarchical authority, and the Panin project was discarded. But the very fact of its even having been set forth shows that the Panin party was not *in principle* opposed to limiting the Crown's power by means of an aristocratic governing body. Evidently the Panin party realized that if some responsible group of this sort did not come into being, then factions coalescing about Catherine's favorites—which in practice meant her lovers—would exercise undue influence, and in an irresponsible manner. Fonvizin and his fellows of the Panin party were always conscious of the perils of favoritism, which they preached and wrote against fervently.

But the central power might be delimited by means other than institutions, no matter how thoroughly formalized they might be. One such means would have been constitutional limitations, in effect, on the authority of the monarch, the definition of certain areas which his power could not reach. Such a notion underlay Fonvizin's work of 1783, the "Discourse on Permanent Laws of the State" (II, 254–67). This essay starts from the doctrine that the monarch is the representative of divine power on earth. It then argues that God, even though almighty, has fixed certain physical and moral laws which He Himself cannot violate; and concludes that a ruler, as His representative on earth, must follow suit in the political sphere by establishing inviolable laws setting bounds to his own authority. If he does not, injustice will reign. "Justice and humility," Fonvizin says (II, 259), are the qualities which demonstrate that a ruler is indeed God's representative on earth and consequently invest him with the Divinity's own authority. To be sure, the earthly ruler enjoys a monopoly of force by which he *may* impose his will even unjustly, but "force coerces, while law [*pravo*] obliges" (II, 263). "True law," Fonvizin continues, "is the one which is recognized by the reason as just and which therefore engenders some sort of internal obligation within us to obey voluntarily" (II, 263). In short, the laws of the state must be in harmony with the laws of reason. If they are, they will be obeyed without the coercive power of the state. In like manner, "constitutional" restrictions upon the monarch's authority should also be consonant with reason, for then the monarch as a human being and his subjects as human beings will accept them as just.

Fonvizin ended his "Discourse" with his favorite phrase: "The first title" of the ruler, he said, "is the title of an honest man . . ." (II, 267).

A few years before, in 1779, Fonvizin had published the *Ta-Gio*, a compilation of advice from the Confucian tradition on how to rule a nation virtuously. "Genuine wisdom," we read there, ". . . consists in loving people and inculcating in them love for virtue . . ." (II, 231). This fits in well with the general argument of the "Discourse" of 1783, since Fonvizin here does not so much prescribe specific laws and limitations as discuss the innate rules of virtue to which the ruler, like all other men, should adhere. Thus the actions of the monarch in the final accounting are to be restricted by the internal limitations of virtue and morality, or of love in the Christian sense rather than law in the Judaic tradition. Much earlier, in his panegyric *Discourse on the Recovery of Paul Petrovich* of 1771, Fonvizin had tendered some advice to the future monarch concerning the ruler and his people. Remember the maternal love which Catherine has shown you in your distress, Fonvizin exhorted Paul, and "love the Russians. You cannot doubt, Sire, their enthusiasm for you. . . . Love them even as you are beloved of them." Then Fonvizin summarized his position in one sentence: "The love of the people is the genuine glory of rulers" (II, 192, 193).

Christian love for others and love of virtue should be the true check on the arbitrary exercise of power, for laws will be of no effect if they are deliberately disregarded. But how is the ruler to acquire an understanding of the laws he should obey? Primarily, it would seem, through education. That was Panin's objective in his efforts to afford Paul the best possible moral and intellectual education. Panin hoped to instil the precepts of morality in his charge forever, so that he would voluntarily observe them when on the throne.

It was also possible that the ruler might seek the counsel of a genuinely moral and virtuous individual, oblivious of his own fate, who would guide him in the proper paths. Such is the subject of Fonvizin's "Greek tale" of 1786, "Callisthenes." Callisthenes is a philosopher and pupil of Aristotle's. Alexander the Great has written Aristotle requesting his former teacher to send him a philosopher as advisor. Callisthenes is understandably reluctant to accept this task, but he also is persuaded that his dedication to truth is sufficiently strong to withstand even the threat of death, so he joins the conquering Alexander in Persia and is received with all possible honors. Soon after his arrival he attends a meeting of Alexander's advisors, who urge him to treat the family of the conquered Darius harshly, but Alexander instead follows Callisthenes's counsel and shows them respect. Shortly thereafter Callisthenes suggests that mercy be granted the inhabitants of a certain region, and again carries the day against Alexander's military advisors.

Soon, however, Callisthenes provokes the opposition of Alexander's corrupt and evil favorite, Leonad, who strives by all possible means to undermine the position of the philosopher, whom he terms a "learned fool." Alexander yields to foul counsel: he fancies himself a god, murders a friend, succumbs to drink, and destroys a city at a whim. Learning of this, Callisthenes penetrates into Alexander's chambers and denounces him to his face as a "monster" "unworthy of the name of man" (II, 38). Alexander thereupon hands Callisthenes over to Leonad to be tortured and executed. Callisthenes is philosophical at the end, and before his death rejoices at the good he accomplished in the two days he enjoyed Alexander's trust.

"Callisthenes" depicts the struggle for the soul of the monarch between the virtuous philosopher-counselor and the evil favorite. At the time he wrote it, apparently, Fonvizin was prey to pessimism, and thought that the latter would invariably prevail over the former. And yet the tale is ultimately optimistic, for Callisthenes's letter to Aristotle argues that it is worth much to sustain good over evil even if only for a short time.

Such was Fonvizin's attitude toward the monarchy more or less in the abstract. In enunciating his views, however, he had always to recall that he was writing during the reign of a very specific monarch who considered herself something of a philosopher and moral law-giver. Soviet scholars ordinarily present Fonvizin as an inveterate opponent of Catherine and her policies except in a few specific cases, but the documents at our disposal indicate that he usually regarded her positively, and sometimes extravagantly positively, even when we make allowances for the flowery style of the eighteenth century in its more solemn moments (many of Fonvizin's letters to highly placed correspondents consist of little more than compliments and elaborate rhetorical formulas). For example, the *Discourse on the Recovery of Paul Petrovich* abounds in praise of Catherine, "child-loving mother and source of our glory and bliss" (II, 187), for her maternal concern both for her son Paul and for the Russian people as a whole. Midway through the work Fonvizin describes a visit by Catherine to her son's sickbed. "Catherine wishes to comfort her son by means of words," Fonvizin wrote, "but tears choke off her words." With an effort she suppresses her grief in Paul's presence, but when she returns to her private apartments her tears flow copiously. "This is the trait of a great soul!" the author exclaims. "Happy is the land in which the ruler controls both his own heart and those of his people" (II, 190). Fonvizin concludes his brochure on Paul's recovery with an apostrophe to Catherine:

Wisdom guides her, successes follow upon her deeds, conquests crown her with laurels, and Russia is glorified by her glory. In her we have our present favor, and in Paul our hope of future bliss (II, 193).

Although Fonvizin had no particular reason to be grateful to Catherine immediately after Panin's resignation in 1781, he still spoke of her very glowingly in his *Life of N. I. Panin* (1784). In describing the many honors she had bestowed upon Panin, he asks that Catherine's "sacred name and magnificent deeds be granted immortality" (II, 281), and he incorporates the text of the letter she wrote Panin upon the occasion of Paul's attaining his majority, when she bestowed her largesse upon him for his services (II, 285).

As late as 1788, before Fonvizin met frustration in his plans to publish a journal comprised of his own writings, he still lauded Catherine extravagantly. He granted particular approbation to her encouragement of freedom of expression, a freedom which concerned Fonvizin directly. In his "Letter to Starodum from the Author of *The Minor*," he makes light of the censor, since the "age of Catherine the Second has been marked by the granting to Russians of the freedom to think and express themselves," in a manner quite unthinkable before she came to the throne (II, 41). In "Starodum's Reply," Starodum agrees entirely with Fonvizin's statement, saying that thirty years before people had avoided even overhearing potentially subversive conversations for fear of the possible consequences. Catherine, by contrast, had permitted the establishment of "free printing presses," which bestowed upon the Russian writer unprecedented liberty and also unprecedented responsibilities, particularly that of "being a useful counselor to the ruler, and sometimes even the savior of his fellow citizens and his Fatherland" (II, 42). All this had come about because Catherine had "struck the fetters from writers' hands."

Moreover, Fonvizin had reason to be grateful to Catherine herself and to those about her at the highest level of government. It was she, after all, who had invited him to read his controversial *The Brigadier* to her personally, and had approved of it. It was her counselor, that powerful statesman Nikita Panin, who had promoted *The Brigadier* among the aristocratic circles of St. Petersburg and even introduced Fonvizin into the circle of the Grand Duke. And it was Potemkin who in 1782 had spoken so highly of *The Minor*, and quite possibly assisted him in having it staged in the capital. By way of contrast, Fonvizin had encountered difficulties with Russian officialdom at a lower level: the Moscow censor had delayed the staging of *The Minor* for some time, and the publication of his prospective journal of 1788 was forbidden by the police despite his protestations of disbelief that such a thing could happen in the age of Catherine the Second.

The most important conflict between Catherine and Fonvizin—one which Soviet scholars invariably mention—occurred with the publication of Fonvizin's "Questions" of 1783, and Catherine's replies. It is beyond dispute that the questions were in some instances phrased exceedingly sharply, and that Catherine was touchy in some of her responses. This was especially so in the case of the famous question 14b, in which Fonvizin asked: "Why is it that in earlier times fools, clowns, and jokers held no ranks, while nowadays they do, and very high ranks at that?" To this Catherine answered, at first gently, that "our ancestors were not literate" (which had little enough to do with the question), then added: "This question springs from *excessive freedom of speech* [*svobodoiazychie*], which our ancestors did not have either" (II, 274).

One may ask precisely what Fonvizin hoped to accomplish by submitting these questions for publication. In many ways, as we have noted, they dealt with a definition of the national character, but as K. A. Papmehl points out in his study of freedom of expression in Russia, they were also a "spectacular example of a conscious practical test of free expression."[4] Papmehl discovered that the Englishman Samuel Bentham, who was at the time close to Princess Dashkova, publisher of the *Sobesednik*, thought Fonvizin quite outspoken, and wrote to his brother in October of 1783 that his questions "would astonish you by their freedom."[5] It is not plain whether Bentham made this statement in an English context or in a purely Russian one, but it is quite reasonable to assume that through his questions Fonvizin was testing the limits of the permissible in the public political discourse of his time. And it developed that his freedom was rather extensive. To be sure, Fonvizin did feel constrained to reply to the replier in his letter "K g. sochiniteliu 'Bylei i nebylits' ot sochinitelia voprosov" (To the Author of "Fact and Fiction" from the Author of the Questions). In this response Fonvizin apologized for some lack of clarity in the formulation of his initial queries. He asserted that he was second to none in his appreciation of the accomplishments of Catherine's reign, and it was for that reason that he was so distressed to see certain members of the nobility transformed into "servile" individuals. He also clarified the wording of some of his other questions, maintaining that he had had nothing insulting in mind. He rejected the charge against him of "excessive freedom of speech," which, he said, he "hated with all his soul" (II, 278). Fonvizin's response was generally conciliatory in tone, but it was no recantation of his views by any reasonable interpretation. Moreover, as a social critic Fonvizin should have anticipated rebuttals to his criticisms in a relatively free press, even if they came from Catherine herself. The important point is that Catherine did not invoke any of the official sanctions against him which she possessed the power to impose. Instead, she respected the principle of freedom of speech, though she insisted that it apply to herself as well, especially when she was writing anonymously.

It is true that some passages in Fonvizin's works lend themselves to the interpretation that he was fiercely opposed to Catherine, and especially to her Court. One such passage occurs at the end of a long conversation between Pravdin and Starodum in the first scene of Act Three of *The Minor*. Here Starodum recalls his experiences at Court, and his decision to leave it for his estate. He believed that the dishonorable flatterers who held the upper hand at the Court would before long purge him, and preferred to depart voluntarily, thus preserving his honor intact. To Pravdin's protestations that men of his quality should be brought to the Court rather than driven from it, just as a "doctor is called in to those who are sick," Starodum replies that "it is vain to summon a doctor to those who are incurably ill. Here a doctor can do no good, but will simply become infected himself" (II, 132–33).

This exchange between Pravdin and Starodum may be understood as an attack on Catherine, but it is even more obviously an assault on the Court and on those attracted to the Court for the sake of personal gain. The holder of supreme power under any political system tends to attract such unworthy people, and it is his responsibility to guard against them. Almost invariably, however, the entire system is established so as to encourage them instead, which means that the system must be altered in major essentials. But the target of Fonvizin's shafts in this passage is more the flatterers, self-seekers, and incompetents who were always the butt of his barbs rather than Catherine herself, or the monarchical system, or those at the height of that system. He was referring to those slightly further down, who did not have the best interests of the nation at heart. Fonvizin sought to hold Catherine to the ideals which she in theory espoused, and with which he agreed, but which were difficult to sustain as a practical political matter.

The difficulties of imagining a social system which rewards virtue and punishes vice instead of the opposite are evident in the final contribution to the *Friend of Honest Men,* entitled "Nastavlenie diadi svoemu plemianniku" (An Uncle's Advice to His Nephew). The uncle in question had in his day been counseled by his dying father to be "goodhearted, charitable, and hard-working." At first he sought to apply this "system" in reality, only to discover that he made enemies by his goodheartedness, piled up debt by being charitable, and as a result of his knowledge "acquired the envy and hatred of a certain important ignoramus, who considered enlightenment harmful to the state" (II, 75). Consequently he resolved to abandon his "system" altogether: he ignored the pleas of the poor, discarded all his books, and married a stupid but beautiful woman through whom he made many friends and soon became wealthy and socially esteemed. However, although the external observer may think him happy and prosperous, now that death is approaching his conscience torments him, and he has again revised his "system," enjoining his nephew to learn from his experience (II, 74–78). This ending appears contrived, an artificial affirmation that the virtuous life is worth living, indeed the only life worth living. But the chief element in this work is the notion of a "system," or set of rules for living. Fonvizin here argues that the nonvirtuous life will lead to social acceptance and riches, but will also engender the pangs of conscience. The task is to arrange society so that the rewards of a virtuous life will be, not only a clear conscience, but also material wealth and social prestige.

II *The Nature of the Good Society*

In addition to formulating—in his translations and original writings—his prescriptions for the ideal monarchical system, Fonvizin also presented his thoughts on the nature of the ideal society and the ideal citizen. Although the individual elements of his viewpoint must be drawn from various sources, they form a relatively coherent whole.[6]

In the first place, the individual must be bound to his society, to his nation, by the bonds of patriotism. This view, implicit or explicit, runs through the travel letters, and in 1785 Fonvizin published a translation on this question, the *Essay on National Patriotism*. Fonvizin was not alone in dealing with this topic, for many other Russian writers of the day, including Radishchev, were seeking to define the national character and the nature of the true "son of the Fatherland," or patriot.

In this essay the author, Johann Georg Zimmermann, argues that the individual must be loyal to ideals beyond himself if he is to accomplish anything of worth; he must not be absorbed merely by his own personal interests. The idea of the nation has traditionally enabled the individual to rise above himself to a conception of the general good. In short, the word *Fatherland* became the "soul of society," as Zimmermann wrote in speaking of the inculcation of patriotism in ancient societies (II, 297).

Aside from patriotism, Fonvizin dealt intermittently with the question of freedom and equality in society, and the appropriate interrelationship between them. In his play *The Selection of a Tutor*, written after the outbreak of the French revolution, Fonvizin emphasizes the complexities of political action. Politics, Nelstetsov argues in that play, is much more complicated than mathematics, where one may build with confidence on that which has been previously established: "The political mind is and has to be incomparably greater, and is encountered much more rarely, than the mathematical mind" (I, 200). And a very thorny question with which the "political mind" had to grapple was that of the linkage between freedom and equality.

Fonvizin strongly favors freedom over equality, in a reaction, no doubt, against French radical extremism. In *The Selection of a Tutor*, Nelstetsov maintains that the ideal of absolute equality is a chimera. There can never be absolute equality between social classes because the nature of reality is such that one class will always be subordinate to another (I, 200). Indeed, Fonvizin was rather a theoretician of the functions of social classes, as we have seen above: he believed there should be distinctions between classes, and, by extension, inequalities between them as well. And the creator of such personages as Skotinin on the one hand and Starodum on the other could only believe that there were vast differences and inequalities between individuals also.

Fonvizin found the subject of freedom more intriguing than equality. In his *"Eulogy of Marcus Aurelius"* (1777), a central precept reads, "Liberty is the first right of man" (*Vol'nost' est' pervoe pravo cheloveka*, II, 212). But the word "liberty" has many meanings, and Fonvizin wished to distinguish them, especially as they applied to civil law. Thus, during his sojourn in Montpellier in 1777–78, he undertook the study of French law, among other things, and summarized his thoughts in an interesting passage from a letter to Peter Panin.

"The first right of every Frenchman is liberty" (II, 460), Fonvizin wrote there, paraphrasing the quotation from the *Eulogy,* and this principle had been incorporated into the system of French law by "rare minds" over many centuries. The structure of the French legal system in theory was admirable in its logic, but in practice "abuses and the deterioration of morals" had weakened its foundations. Its present condition seemed irreparable to Fonvizin, who wrote that "It is terrible to live in it but fatal to detroy it." Fonvizin's final analysis of the condition of freedom in France is strikingly similar to that which the radical Alexander Herzen, an émigré from his native land, would advance in opposition to Western bourgeois freedoms more than seventy years later:

The first right of every Frenchman is liberty; but his actual condition at the moment is slavery, for a poor man cannot feed himself except by slave labor, and if he should really want to exercise his precious liberty, he would die of hunger. In short, the word liberty is devoid of any meaning, and the right of the strong remains superior to any law. (II, 460)

Fonvizin contrasted the formal freedom and actual enserfment to economic necessity of the Frenchman to the formal enserfment and actual freedom of the Russian peasant. The important thing for him was the actual condition of the citizen, and not the formal rights which he supposedly possessed.

Still, Fonvizin did not reject the idea of freedom in the formal sense entirely. David Ransel believes that the Panin party felt any move toward the abolition of serfdom would lead to greater upheavals than Russian society could sustain.[7] But Fonvizin—at least early on, before the outbreak of the Pugachev rebellion—thought otherwise. He ended his "Extract on the Freedom of the French Nobility" (1764–66) by recommending that Russia have a peasantry nourished by at least the hope of ultimate liberation (II, 116). And he supported the viewpoint of the Panin party that, even though any elimination of serfdom might be long in coming, for the present serfowners should not be permitted to violate human decency in their relationships with their serfs. During the great legislative commission convened by Catherine in 1767–68, any mention of possible regulation of the master-serf relationship by the highest state authorities aroused vigorous opposition from all but a few of the gentry deputies.[8] But Fonvizin and his political allies held that the central government had every right to uphold the natural laws of humanity, even to the extent of depriving serfowners of their property rights. That, after all, was the chief political message of *The Minor*. When Prostakova refers to the "liberty" *(vol' nost')* which the nobility is supposed to enjoy, she is informed in no uncertain terms that liberty does not extend to tyranny.

As a writer, Fonvizin was especially concerned with freedom of expression. The satirical journals of 1769 and the early 1770s extended freedom of expression, and we have already seen that Fonvizin sought to expand its limits even further in his exchanges of 1783 with Catherine. One may surmise that during the 1780s he referred so constantly to the freedom of expression which Catherine had granted her people in order to remind her of her own ideals and cause her to sustain them. In his "Letter from Starodum" he speculates on the reasons for the lack of oratorical talent in contemporary Russia and decides that it must be rooted in "a lack of situations in which the gift of eloquence might be exhibited" (II, 64). Starodum then suggests that the Russian Academy encourage public speaking and debate through oratorical competitions. That never occurred, but the very proposal illustrates the weight which Fonvizin attached to intellectually free and vigorous discussion of questions of public policy. One could, he thought, preach to the mighty of this world if one were sufficiently discreet about it.

As a nobleman, Fonvizin was concerned—along with other writers of his time, such as Derzhavin—with the rights and especially the obligations of the gentry class. As Seum comments in *The Selection of a Tutor*, despite the views of most of the gentry class, nobility should not be purely hereditary. The nobleman as an individual should possess qualities of soul defining him as noble, including particularly a "desire to be useful to his Fatherland" (I, 191), a patriotic sense of duty. The serfs were under both a legal and a moral obligation to their masters; the nobility had gradually emancipated itself from many of the legal requirements of service, but this meant that it sustained an even heavier moral responsibility to be of use to the state. "I don't know of anything lower in this world," Starodum exclaims in *The Minor*, than a "nobleman unworthy of the name" (I, 153). And a nobleman worthy of the name is ever conscious of his "duty."

Starodum expands upon his concept of duty in *The Minor* by recounting the tale of a certain count, a very intelligent and well-educated man, whom he had known in his youth. When war broke out, Starodum welcomed the opportunity to serve his Fatherland, but the count felt he could not be spared at home. Starodum served valiantly at war, but while he was recovering from his wounds his former friend the count, safe at home, was unjustly promoted (I, 130–31). Not only was this "nobleman" morally deficient, then, but he was also rewarded for that deficiency.

Another attribute of the truly noble man should be bravery, bravery not just in the physical sense, but in the moral sense especially. The soldier Milon emphasizes this point in *The Minor* when he says he has not yet discovered whether he is truly brave, although he has frequently been in battle. For then he was but a subordinate, obliged to carry out orders bravely. A commander, on the other hand, must prefer "his reputation to his life," and, more important, the reputation of his country to his own reputation. And bravery is by no means limited to the military, by any means: a high degree of it is required in the civilian official who dares to tell his sovereign the truth at the risk of arousing his anger, and perhaps losing his position. That sort of bravery, Milon asserts, is markedly rarer than the bravery of the duellist, and he employs different Russian words to denote them (I, 157–58). The valor of those who accept responsibility for the fate of their society is a major contribution to the good of the state. Fonvizin thought Panin exhibited that virtue, and he strove to exercise it himself.

Most of the desirable qualities of the nobleman could be subsumed under the concept of "virtue," one of Fonvizin's central ideas. In his study of literature and political philosophy among those he calls the Fonvizin group of the 1760s (Ippolit Bogdanovich, Novikov, Lukin, and Fonvizin), Walter Gleason shows that in the earlier period as well Fonvizin was primarily concerned with questions of a moral order, and hoped to redeem and reform society from within rather than from without.[9] That same sort of concern remained uppermost in Fonvizin's mind constantly. Thus in 1772 he wrote to Peter Panin in this same spirit, saying that it was better to be without education than be given a corrupted one, adding that "a virtuous heart is a man's greatest value, and bliss in our life is to be sought and found only in it" (II, 377). At the beginning of Act Four of *The Minor*, Starodum finds Sofya reading a work on the education of girls by the seventeenth-century French moralist François Fénelon, whom he contrasts approvingly with the contemporary French encyclopedists. The latter, he says, "uproot prejudices very thoroughly, but they are eradicating virtue at the same time" (I, 150). Starodum then elaborates upon his notion of the relationship between the intellectual and moral:

Intellect, if no more than that, is nothing at all. It is easy to find bad husbands, bad fathers, and bad citizens with brilliant minds. Only virtue can give true worth to the intellect. Without it, an intelligent man is a monster. (I, 152)

An "honest man" is a beacon for society, an ideal toward which others should strive.

Just as virtue should be the lodestar of the individual in society, so also should it be the cement of that basic social structure, the family. The question of the family, as we have seen, was a central one in *The Brigadier*, although in a more tragicomic sense, and Fonvizin returns to it more systematically in *The Minor*. The conversation between Sofya and Starodum in Act Four of *The Minor* consists in large measure of Starodum's disquisitions on the family, since his niece is about to assume family responsibilities. The chief question to be asked about a marriage, says Starodum, is not whether the man is wealthy, or the woman beautiful, but whether both walk in the ways of virtue. He paints a repulsive picture of the contemporary family, in which the husband is a "coarse and dissolute tyrant," the wife exhibits "willful impudence," and neither provides any moral standards for their unfortunate children (I, 153–54). Displaying his usual fondness for bipartite generalizations, Starodum argues that husband and wife should feel, not "love which resembles friendship," but "friendship which resembles love," and which will remain constant over all the years of their marriage (I, 154–55). In Starodum's view, the wife must be subordinate to her husband as the head of the family, but he must in turn adhere to the dictates of right reason, and then their marital union will be entirely happy (I, 155).

A modicum of tension on this issue is introduced into the play for a time when Count Chestan writes to Starodum of the marriage proposal Milon has made to Sofya. Starodum interviews Milon and is wholly pleased with his moral character; thereafter he is even more delighted to discover that Sofya has already given her heart to Milon. "What's this?" Starodum exclaims. "Your heart has already sought out the man I was suggesting for you? This is the man I wanted you to marry . . ." (I, 158). Thus it develops that when the traditional forms are infused with moral virtue, the wishes of a girl's heart will coincide with the rational judgment of her guardian, and no true conflict can ensue between love and filial duty. Under such circumstances, Starodum immediately assents to the marriage. At the conclusion of Act Four, it is not Sofya but Starodum who rejects the suits of both Mitrofan and Skotinin on her behalf (I, 165).

Although it might appear that no couple could be more devoted to virtue than Sofya and Milon, with the passage of time even such ideal heroes have their troubles. One of the items to have been published in *The Friend of Honest Men* for 1788 was a letter from Sofya to Starodum, in which she tells her uncle that, after several years of marriage and a move to St. Petersburg, Milon has betrayed her with a painted woman. Sofya still loves Milon deeply, and suffers pangs of jealousy; she begs her uncle's advice as to her course of action at this critical juncture (II, 43). Starodum sends a reply which reduces to a lengthy exhortation to patience. Everything will pass, he assures her; a "virtuous wife must bear the madness of her husband patiently" (II, 44). Your rival is clearly such a despicable woman that it is a shame to be jealous over her. "Be patient and magnanimous," is his concluding counsel (II, 45). Virtue will prevail, and will sustain the ideal of the family.

Such, then, was the character of the good society as Fonvizin envisioned it. The cornerstone of the structure was virtue rather than freedom, although the latter was essential too. The nobleman will fulfil his duties to the state and his responsibilities to his serfs, if he is virtuous; a wife will forgive her husband's misdeeds, and he will repent of them, if both are virtuous; the blessings of true freedom—

and not merely the formal guarantees of Western legislation—will accrue to all members of society if all are virtuous, or at least if the political leadership structures the society so as to reward good and punish evil. Fonvizin would have Russia become first a virtuous society, secondarily a free one, and not a particularly egalitarian one.

III   *Politics and Satire*

Fonvizin's devotion to social ideals and his pitiless analyses of existing reality led him on the one hand toward didacticism, and on the other toward satire, two strands inextricably intertwined in *The Minor*. Indeed, both of these strands coexist in most of his original writing, with now one, now the other predominant.

A brief work of Fonvizin's which emphasizes the didactic to the virtual exclusion of the satirical is the "Pouchenie, govorennoe v Dukhov den' " (Sermon for the Feast of the Holy Spirit [the Monday after Pentecost], II, 24–27), published in the *Sobesednik* in 1783. In this form the "Sermon" represents an unusual genre for Fonvizin, although it may be linked to his apparent interest in certain older forms of Russian literature, especially the sermons so prominent in Old Russian literature immediately after the Christianization of Russia in the late tenth century. This particular sermon, supposedly preached by the village priest Vasily, moves on no lofty rhetorical or theological level. It is a simple sermon preached to simple peasants to promulgate a simple Christian ethic of dedication to work and avoidance of drunkenness. The preacher assumes a direct connection between the pursuit of virtue and the material blessings accruing to the individual as he holds members of his congregation up to censure or praise. Yakov Lysoy, he says, has always been lazy and good for nothing, and now he begs at the church gate. But Yakov Alekseev has a large and loving family who have served their country well and are a model for us all (II, 26). The sermon is very much tailored to the needs of a particular congregation, indeed so much so that perhaps we should take seriously the author's introductory footnote, where he says he heard the sermon delivered and asked Father Vasily to record it for him. This might explain the fact that the "Sermon" is so out of character for Fonvizin.

A more interesting example of Fonvizin's prose of 1783 is the *Tale of a Pretended Deaf-Mute*, in which Fonvizin announced that his objective was "to gain an acquaintance with people and gain an acquaintance with man" (II, 12). The best path to this end was for the narrator to pretend, at his father's urging, to have become both deaf and dumb as a result of illness, so that people will speak so freely in his presence as to display their true thoughts and motivations. The kernel idea is ingenious, but Fonvizin hardly begins to exploit it properly in the fragment which he published in the *Sobesednik:* only toward the conclusion does the youthful narrator begin to observe things which he otherwise would have missed. Until that point, Fonvizin creates an entertaining series of Russian types, for example the "religious hypocrite" Varukh Yazvin, who drove to Rostov with stolen horses to pray for his sins (II, 15–16), or Mikhey Antifonov, who declined to take medicines in his illness but insistently treated himself with wine (II, 15–16). To a degree the *Tale* foreshadows the work a century later of Nikolay Leskov, who would endow Russian literature with a richly elaborated collection of rogues and Russian types. Fonvizin's *Tale* remained an unfinished but still entertaining narrative effort.

The satirical strand is prominent in the only original verse fable to reach us from Fonvizin's pen, "Lisitsa-Kaznodei" (The Preacher Fox, I, 207–208), written in verse which even the hypercritical Vladimir Nabokov pronounced "excellent."[10] The date of this work's composition is uncertain. Most Fonvizin specialists have dated it 1762, but L. I. Kulakova has argued—convincingly, in my view, if only because the fable is of such high quality that one can hardly imagine a seventeen-year-old beginner's having written it—that it should be dated between 1782 and 1787, in which latter year it was first published.[11]

"The Preacher Fox" is set in the faraway land of Libya, after the death of King Lion. The Fox ascends the pulpit to eulogize the departed ruler as the "tsar wisest of all tsars of the forest," "father to his servants," etc. The Fox works himself up into an "ecstasy" of self-humiliation, and much of the sermon's phraseology is reminiscent of the famous eulogy preached by Feofan Prokopovich upon Peter the Great's death. The voice of truth in the fable is that of the Mole, who assures the Dog that the Fox's praise is false: the Lion had been a genuine "swine," under whose rule the animals had known only suffering; one honest artist had starved to death only a few days earlier. When the Mole expresses his astonishment at the Fox's enthusiastic flattery, the Dog replies that any animal who has lived among mankind would find this entirely natural, for flattery is the path of advancement for the unscrupulous and low individual.

The satirical strain clearly prevails over the didactic one in

Fonvizin's fiction of the later 1780s, and most especially in several of the works designed for publication in *The Friend of Honest Men*. One of his most entertaining satires was cast in a superficially unpromising form, that of a grammar.

The author prefaces his brief "Vseobshchaia pridvornaia grammatika" (Universal Courtiers' Grammar) with a short foreword disclaiming any topical significance for it, since, we are told, the manuscript was discovered in Asia, where Courts are said to have first arisen, and dates from shortly after the Flood (II, 47). The body of the "Grammar" is arranged like a catechism, with questions and answers, and relies heavily upon puns (which, by the way, also supply most of the humor in Mitrofan's grammar examination in *The Minor*). The "Courtiers' Grammar," we learn, is "the science of flattering slily with tongue and pen," a science whose rules may be codified (II, 48). Fonvizin's classifications are humorous by their sheer absurdity: for example, words at Court are grouped as monosyllabic (yes, prince, slave), disyllabic (mighty, fallen), trisyllabic (merciful), and multisyllabic (the Russian word for "highness," II, 49).

Individual vowels and consonants have meaning at Court. If a powerful personage says "O!" upon receiving a report from a subordinate, then the situation is hopeless; but if the same question is interpreted for him in such a fashion that he perceives his initial mistake, he may say "A!" and the problem may be resolved. The tense system also has its functions at Court: most petitions to the mighty employ the past tense ("I have served my country"), while most replies of the mighty utilize the future tense ("We shall see"). The verbal construction most frequently employed at Court is "to be in debt." It is rarely used in the past tense since nobody ever pays his debts (II, 50–51).

Fonvizin employed another unlikely vessel, a brief bureaucratic register, to bear satirical content also. The "Register" (II, 53–54) consists of a series of requests to a high official for favorable decisions on various cases, and includes information on what a favorable decision would be worth to each petitioner. In his "Otvet" (Response, II, 55–57), the official does indeed reach favorable decisions, although in one case he mentions his need of more "documents" than the 500 (rubles) already provided him.

Pushkin thought very highly of another of Fonvizin's satires, the "Razgovor u kniagini Khaldinoi" (Conversation at Princess Khaldina's). This conversation among Zdravomysl, the judge Sorvantsov, and Princess Khaldina, which takes place in the latter's boudoir, analyzes with wit and intelligence a whole gamut of social and individual vices (II, 65–74). The topics under discussion include education, gambling, official corruption, religious hypocrisy, and several others. Written in Fonvizin's finest colloquial style, the "Conversation" is fundamentally satirical, although it is undergirded by didacticism in assuming the desirability of that which a Starodum had preached in the past and a Nelstetsov would preach in the future. It also exemplifies Fonvizin's predilection for the monologue or dialogue as a literary form: his was preeminently the conversational rather than the descriptive voice. Add to this his preference for fragmentary forms—especially strong toward the end of his life—and the "Conversation" emerges as a highly characteristic Fonvizinian work.

CHAPTER 7

Fonvizin and the History of the Russian Literary Language

I *A Confusion of Tongues*

AS with several other aspects of Fonvizin's life and work, scholars
have disagreed over the decades about the quality of his
contribution to the development of the Russian literary language of
the eighteenth century.

His first biographer, Vyazemsky, believed Fonvizin had failed to
cope with the confusions of the literary language at his disposal; he
could not control the Church Slavic and French influences impinging
upon his Russian,[1] and therefore his language was a chaotic
hodgepodge. Later in his study, to be sure, Vyazemsky credited
Fonvizin with initiating a "revolution" *(perevorot)* in the literary
language, which, however, only Karamzin had brought to fruition.
Fonvizin was inferior to Karamzin, in Vyazemsky's opinion, in that
the latter developed and improved his writing abilities systematically
over his lifetime, whereas no such development was visible in
Fonvizin: with him all depended upon the inspiration of the moment.[2]

Fonvizin's reputation as a molder of the literary language improved
to a degree at the end of the nineteenth century. In 1894 Vladimir
Istomin published a major article on his language,[3] and in 1904 K.P.
Petrov dedicated to him one of the first dictionaries of the language of
an individual writer ever published.[4] Such attention indicates that at
that time he began to be thought a moderately important figure in the
history of the Russian literary language, and in the decades since then
Russian scholars have published occasional specialized articles on
aspects of his language.

In the general histories of the Russian literary language,
however—for example those by Alexander Efimov or Viktor
Vinogradov—Fonvizin is accorded a secondary place, bracketed

briefly between Lomonosov and Karamzin. At most only a few pages will be devoted to his place in the development of the literary language, and this is in fact more or less what he deserves. Fonvizin did not make the contributions to linguistic theory of a Lomonosov, nor was he nearly so exemplary in his literary practice as Karamzin. Nevertheless, he did contribute to the development of the literary language in ways which deserve some mention.

In Fonvizin's day writers faced the task of integrating several major strands within a single literary language. The foundation of that language was the Russian spoken by the intelligentsia. It was heavily penetrated, however, by other linguistic influences. One was Church Slavic, the ecclesiastical language common to all the Slavic Orthodox churches, including the Russian Orthodox. A second was the so-called "Chancery language," the jargon of the civil and military bureaucracy. And a third was contemporary Western languages, including German but especially French, the first language of much of the Russian aristocracy. All these influences affected the lexicon and syntax of the Russian literary language, of which Fonvizin's language is an important part.

The question of the proper relationship between Church Slavic and Russian was not satisfactorily resolved until Pushkin's time, or even somewhat thereafter. Fonvizin was thoroughly familiar with Church Slavic, and commented in his autobiography that "it is impossible even to know the Russian language without it" (II, 87). He was raised in a pious household where the feasts of the Church were carefully observed, and often read from Scripture for services at home, so that he absorbed the ecclesiastical language naturally. Church Slavic for the educated Russian of that day performed a role similar to that of "King James English" for the cultured English speaker of our day: it was seriously employed in speaking of elevated subjects, as Lomonosov had prescribed in his theory of the "three styles," the most famous eighteenth-century attempt to define the proper place of Church Slavic in the Russian literary language. Fonvizin's penchant for Church Slavic—although we possess no direct evidence for this—must have been reinforced by his association with Ivan Elagin during the 1760s. Elagin has been termed a forerunner of the Slavophiles in his emphasis upon the linguistic importance of Church Slavic; his Slavic slant emerged very strongly much later, in 1790, in a history of Russia down to 1389.[5]

Fonvizin adopted more or less the solution to the problem of Church Slavic in the Russian literary language suggested by Lomonosov: he used it primarily at serious moments and for elevated discussions. He made one of his few theoretical statements on Church Slavic in the translator's foreward to his version of *Joseph* (1769), a book written on a topic both elevated and edifying. He begins by postulating a rather drastic division between Russian and Church Slavic when he asserts that "all our books have been written either in Slavic or in the contemporary language" (I, 443): in fact most were written in some combination of the two. Then he adds that translations of books on elevated topics, such as *Joseph*,

should strive only for the solemnity of the Slavic language, while at the same time observing the clarity of our language; for though the Slavic language is clear enough in itself, this is only for those who have studied it especially. Consequently, the [literary] language should be of a sort which we do not yet possess. (I, 443)

Ideally, this passage would seem to say, the "solemn" spirit of Church Slavic should be joined to the lexical clarity of contemporary Russian. Fonvizin did not achieve such a synthesis in his translation of *Joseph*, which utilizes not only the recondite syntax of the ecclesiastical language, but also many lexical items not easily understandable to the ordinary educated Russian. Tikhonravov was sufficiently irritated by it all to speak of the language of that translation as a "strange mixture," "lifeless and inorganic."[6] The influence of Church Slavic is even more pronounced in Fonvizin's brochure on the recovery of Grand Duke Paul in 1771: an ecclesiastic of the time might have envied such a solemn and thoroughly Slavonicized style.

Probably Fonvizin's final word on the synthesis of Russian with Church Slavic is embodied in the *Life of N. I. Panin* of 1784. The topic was certainly serious, and the writer's attitude toward his subject reverential, but the vocabulary of the work is much less heavily Church Slavic than that of the 1771 brochure. There are elevated words in plenty throughout it, but they are for the most part recognizably Russian words, often related to the chancery language. Fonvizin captures the "solemnity" of Church Slavic through the length and syntactic complexity of his sentences (although here he may also have drawn upon Latin syntax, where word order was relatively unimportant because of the language's highly inflected character). One rather extreme example from Panin's *Life* may serve to illustrate this: "*Imperatritsa po predstavleniiu kantslera sudila byt' sposobnym grafa Panina k okazaniiu takovoi otechestvu uslugi*" (II, 280–81: The Empress, after the Chancellor's presentation, judged

Count Panin to be capable of performing such service for the Fatherland). Fonvizin here attained the effect of solemnity by using less ordinary—though still Russian—vocabulary, and long, syntactically convoluted sentences.

Fonvizin did respect the ecclesiastical milieu, but he was not averse to employing Church Slavic for satirical purposes with two of his memorable characters: the Counsellor from *The Brigadier*, and the tutor Kuteykin from *The Minor*. Both men are morally unworthy and very poor representatives of the religious person, but they are so steeped in the outward ecclesiastical culture that they can speak in no other language but Church Slavic. Fonvizin evidently considered the use of Church Slavic as a spoken language rather than a written language to be an affectation, and therefore lampooned it in his plays.

As a high-level official for much of his life, Fonvizin had the opportunity to become quite familiar with the language of the bureaucracy as well as the ecclesiastical language. Innumerable state documents passed through his hands, and he could scarcely have avoided their linguistic influence altogether. From time to time elements of the chancery language appeared in the writing, say, of his travel letters, although these on the whole provide one of the very best examples of the colloquial literary Russian of his day. Fonvizin also parodied the language of the bureaucracy in *The Brigadier*: the vocabulary of the civil bureaucracy through the Counsellor, and the vocabulary of the military through the Brigadier.

Fonvizin had difficulty in combating contemporary foreign influences on the language. The outright use of French—as in the dialogues of Ivanushka and the Counsellor's wife in *The Brigadier*—was easy to attack, and Fonvizin did so unmercifully, although he himself quoted from French and other foreign languages frequently enough. Curiously, Fonvizin incorporated French syntactic calques (grammatical constructions taken over from French) most extensively in the language of his positive characters such as Starodum, Milon, Pravdin, and Sofya from *The Minor*, rather than his negative ones. Strycek lists numerous French syntactic calques found in the speeches of these characters.[7] In his travel letters, where Fonvizin is writing as himself, he employs French syntactic calques heavily in compliments and polite formulas. Thus one can only conclude that, for Fonvizin, the language of the intelligent and cultured Russian included a fairly high proportion of French syntactic calques. Karamzin, by the way, arrived at much the same synthesis, although he was a bit more subtle about it than Fonvizin.

Fonvizin also employed German syntactic calques on occasion—especially when he placed an infinitive before the main verb at the end of a sentence—but French remained supreme in this regard.

The personages who employ genuine colloquial Russian in Fonvizin's world are representatives of the lower classes—servants such as Eremeevna or Trishka in *The Minor*—or unintelligent or reprehensible individuals, such as the Brigadier's wife in *The Brigadier*, or any of the Prostakov family or Skotinin in *The Minor*. If the very bland language of Starodum or Sofya fits with their abstract character, the colloquial language of the Prostakovs helps remove them from the realm of caricature toward straightforward Realism. Grigory Gukovsky waxed almost lyrical in maintaining that Fonvizin's language led him inevitably in that direction: "Fonvizin was entranced by the colloquial language," Gukovsky wrote, "and this was precisely the path toward Realism in this particular area."[8]

Fonvizin's travel letters presumably provide the best example of what the writer thought good literary Russian should be. His letters to his relatives are composed in a vigorous style, with temperate use of the popular language in proverbs and sayings. His syntax is relatively simple and clear; his vocabulary is accessible; he displays a considerable narrative gift and an eye for the humorous both in foreign cultures and in his own. Though they are a trifle archaic by now, the travel letters display the author's linguistic individuality much better than the Neoclassical bombast of a Lomonosov or the Sentimentalist cliches of a Karamzin. By his bland though skillful style, Karamzin guided the development of the Russian literary language away from Fonvizin's individualism, an individualism which would not be recaptured until Pushkin achieved a basic synthesis of the literary language. A careful investigation might very well show that Fonvizin contributed more to that Pushkinian synthesis than has heretofore been suspected.

II *Fonvizin and Russian Lexicography*

Fonvizin was not a systematic soul. His original works were usually short, even a little journalistic, although he spent considerable time over them. That characteristic disinclination to see things through is observable in his contribution to the history of Russian lexicography.

Fonvizin must have conceived an interest in lexicography at least by the time of his journey to France in 1777. With the French Academy considering the nurture of the French literary language to be one of its chief tasks, the French were leaders in this area. Fonvizin evidently acquired French dictionaries and related reference works from time to time, apparently intending to use them for the promotion of Russian lexicography. In January 1778 we find him writing from Montpellier to a friend about a "lexicon" which another friend of theirs was compiling, but which was proceeding at a disappointingly slow pace (II, 493).

This is all we hear from Fonvizin on the subject of lexicography until he became a founding member of the Russian Academy in October 1783.[9] Evidently Fonvizin had given some thought to the problem of a comprehensive dictionary of the Russian language, for very soon after the Russian Academy's founding, on November 11, 1783, he presented his "Outline for the Compilation of an Interpretive Dictionary of the Slavo-Russian Language" (I, 240–47: note that now Slavic and Russian seem to be a sort of hybrid language rather than two distinct ones, as he had held earlier). The "Outline" was a technical document dealing with words to be excluded; grammatical, etymological, and other information to be provided in each entry; and the definition of each word. Fonvizin proposed that the dictionary be arranged etymologically, with words grouped in nests about their roots, though he also suggested the reader be provided with an alphabetical listing giving the precise location of each word.

Another document of about this time on the same topic was the "Sposob, koim rabota tolkovogo slovaria slaviano-rossiiskogo iazyka skoree i udobnee proizvodit'sia mozhet" (Method of Most Quickly and Efficiently Carrying Out the Work of Compiling a Dictionary of the Slavo-Russian Language, I, 248–51). In this brief work Fonvizin lists already existing dictionaries which should be used in putting the new reference work together, strongly recommends the culling of words from compilations and other works of Old Russian literature, and makes various practical suggestions for organizing the work of compiling the dictionary. Among recent writers he mentions only Sumarokov and Lomonosov as possible sources (I, 249); and indeed, when the dictionary appeared, by far the greatest number of citations (833) came from Lomonosov, with only thirty taken from Sumarokov.[10] That is some indication of the relative esteem in which the two were held at the time.

Although Fonvizin was only one of five members of the dictionary committee, he probably was the one most interested in it at that point, and so his proposals for the dictionary were accepted on November 18 with only minor emendations. But the historian Ivan

Boltin—also a member of the Academy, and also interested in the dictionary—was absent on that occasion, and he differed with Fonvizin on many points. Later, when Fonvizin was in Moscow, the Academy at Boltin's prodding largely reversed its initial acceptance of Fonvizin's suggestions at a meeting of January 30, 1784.

Fonvizin was upset when he learned of this action, and rebutted Boltin's arguments point by point in a lengthy and detailed letter to a St. Petersburg friend (I, 252–59). In particular, Fonvizin pointed out that a dictionary arranged on the etymological principle could be easily transformed into an analogical dictionary if necessary, whereas the converse was not the case (I, 259). The upshot of this exchange was that the Russian Academy once again reversed itself. At a meeting of March 12, 1784, it accepted Fonvizin's plan once more, and the way was clear for work on the dictionary to commence.

Some forty-seven out of sixty members of the Academy, mostly literary figures, assisted in the work of compiling the dictionary. Fonvizin also contributed. As early as January of 1784, before the temporary rejection of his outline for the dictionary, he had written to Princess Dashkova from Moscow, enclosing a list of words beginning with the letters K and L, a list of words which he had culled from a Chronicle, a nest of words derived from the root "to give," and a group of hunting terms elicited from Count Peter Panin, who was apparently something of a specialist in this field (II, 497).

So far as we know, Fonvizin's direct contribution to the *Academy Dictionary* went no further than this, but he always encouraged the project. When the first edition of the *Dictionary* came out from 1789 to 1794, it was arranged on the etymological principle, as Fonvizin had urged, although the second edition (1806–22) jettisoned this approach. The *Academy Dictionary* was the first extensive dictionary of the Russian literary language, a true pioneer in the history of Russian lexicography. And Fonvizin must be credited with providing the theoretical and organization impetus for it. That in itself was no mean accomplishment.

Fonvizin was also a temporary pioneer in the lexicographical subfield of synonyms. In 1783 he published—once more in the *Sobesednik*—his "Opyt rossiiskogo soslovnika" (Preliminary Russian Synonym Dictionary, I, 223–36). Fonvizin's work drew heavily, and without acknowledgment, upon a similar French dictionary by Abbé Girard, and several of Fonvizin's synonym groups were derived almost directly from Girard, although it is impossible to depend entirely on a synonym dictionary in one language for a similar reference book in another. Fonvizin's "Synonym Dictionary" includes primarily verbs and nouns, and exhibits no particular principle of selection. He attempts to distinguish shades of meaning among synonyms, ordinarily providing examples of usage, frequently aphoristic in character. His examples often enough have a political coloration, so that even a linguistic reference work becomes a didactic instrument as well. At times the political thrust of the examples is critical of the established order, but at other times it is not: cf. "Disobedience to superiors is a *crime*" (I, 226). Fonvizin draws extensively upon Church books for his material, and the longest entry —on *"um, razum"* (intellect)—contains philosophical and philological observations before concluding with a brief narrative (I, 231–33).

Linguistic questions could arouse deep passions in the eighteenth century, and Fonvizin's "Synonym Dictionary" was soon attacked in the pages of the *Sobesednik*. He took the criticism rather badly, and replied to it in a "Primechanie na kritiku" (Note on Criticism, I, 237–39), in which he turned the edge of his sarcasm against his critic. The note also included an interesting essay on the concept of a synonym: synonyms were not two or more words meaning exactly the same thing and therefore interchangeable, he wrote: "Do you mean to contend that an abundance of words constitutes the wealth of a language?" Instead, synonyms bore different connotations, and the synonym dictionary should make those connotations explicit, he argued. This passage, though stimulating, turns out to have been borrowed directly from the Abbé Girard.[11]

As usual, Fonvizin did not pursue his pioneering effort with synonyms: he simply broadcast his spiritual seed and hoped it would bear fruit in others. In the case of lexicography proper he has been fortunate, for the Russians, especially in the Soviet period, have published some excellent dictionaries of the Russian language. In the area of synonyms, however, he has fared less well, for general Russian-Russian dictionaries are unsatisfactory in their treatment of synonyms, and special synonym dictionaries have only recently begun to be compiled for Russian in a serious way.

CHAPTER 8

Fonvizin and Russian Literature

I Before Pushkin

AT a remove of two centuries, Fonvizin scarcely remains a vital literary influence in his native land. That role is reserved for the towering figures of world literature, and no Russian author of the eighteenth century has attained that status. Fonvizin is, however, undoubtedly a classic now, and for some time after his death he did exert a living influence on Russian literature, particularly the Russian theater.

Fonvizin's impact on the theater during the quarter-century immediately following the appearance of *The Minor* was, as we have seen, substantial, but it was felt by authors and works which have not survived in the history of Russian literature. His influence on the leading figures of that period was negligible. Derzhavin had his own individual approach to literature, as did Radishchev; and Karamzin and the other representatives of the Sentimentalist or Preromantic school were not in sympathy with his sarcastic and straightforward approach to reality.

Fonvizin became influential with major Russian writers from about 1815 to 1850, during which years several collected editions of his work were published. Alexander Pushkin early acknowledged Fonvizin's accomplishments: although he is ordinarily thought of as a Romantic, there was a Neoclassical strain within him, and a strong sense of the incongruity of much in this life which drew him toward Fonvizin. One of Pushkin's earlier efforts, written while he was still at the Lyceum in Tsarskoe Selo, was the satirical poem *Ten' Fon-Vizina* (Fonvizin's Shade, 1815). Working in a contemporary tradition which included Konstantin Batyushkov's *Videnie na beregakh Lety* (Visions on the Shores of Lethe, 1809), Pushkin envisioned Fonvizin as returning to earth to visit various poets. The interval between his death and his return was so short that he could call upon several

130

authors whom he had known in life. These include Dmitry Khvostov, untalented brother of the lackluster author of a satirical poem directed against him, who was still producing reams of verse to no perceptible avail, and Gavriil Derzhavin. Both Fonvizin and his classical companion Hermes are disappointed by the rhetorical hollowness of Derzhavin's poetry written during the Napoleonic wars, and Hermes comments that Derzhavin has suffered from living much too long (he would die quite soon thereafter, in 1816). Finally, Fonvizin visits Batyushkov, who should have been his literary heir had he not given himself over to hedonistic sloth. Fonvizin concludes that Russian literature will never progress so long as nonentities like Khvostov continue to labor diligently and poets like Batyushkov squander their gifts.

Fonvizin's Shade was a youthful effort of no great consequence for Pushkin, but he always remained an admirer of Fonvizin's work without overestimating its importance, and was constantly attracted to the man he himself characterized as "the scourge and terror of ignoramuses."[1] Pushkin gave him pride of place in the history of the Russian theater in the famous passage from Book One of *Eugene Onegin*, which makes it evident that Pushkin considered him the witty and brilliant founder of Russian comedy. Also Petr Vyazemsky was a member of Pushkin's circle, and when he began his researches on Fonvizin as early as 1821 (though his book was not published until 1848), he must have stimulated Pushkin's interest in Fonvizin even further. One can find references to Fonvizin and—more important—echoes of his work scattered throughout Pushkin's correspondence, critical fragments, and poetry. Pushkin was not fundamentally a comic writer, but he had a sophisticated sense of humor which found nourishment in the playwright's works.

II *After Pushkin*

"The scourge of ignoramuses," the young Pushkin had called Fonvizin, and he was indeed viewed by many in the 1820s as a man of intellect frustrated by the stupidity of society. This partial truth helped to lay the groundwork for the next great achievement of the Russian theater after *The Minor*, Alexander Griboedov's classic play in verse *Gore ot uma* (Woe from Wit, 1829). In *Woe from Wit* the highly intelligent hero, Chatsky, finds himself entirely out of place upon returning to Moscow society after a three-year absence. Discovering that the girl he loves prefers the vapidities of established society to his mordant wit (although she is not stupid either, and has her reasons), Chatsky deserts this social circle in disgust and departs.

Although we have no documentary evidence to prove it, Griboedov surely must have known Fonvizin's work well, and it must have had at least an indirect influence upon the composition of his masterpiece. *The Minor* and *Woe from Wit* were soon linked in the minds of others, in any case, as we know from a discarded version of the fifty-first stanza of Book Seven of *Eugene Onegin:*

> How vividly did caustic Griboedov
> describe the grandsons in a satire .
> just as Fonvizin had described the grandfathers. [2]

Pushkin's reference here to "grandsons" and "grandfathers" implicitly points to the greater resemblance among the negative facets of established society as depicted in the two plays than among the positive ones. As the most vivid characters from *The Minor* remain the Prostakovs and their ilk, so *Woe from Wit* is remembered for the Famusovs and Molchalins, and Chatsky largely to the extent that he criticizes the society they dominate. The positive prescriptions of the two authors differ markedly, if indeed Griboedov may be said to offer any positive prescriptions at all.

The negative aspects of *The Minor* remained almost exclusively in the mind of one of Russia's greatest writers, Nikolay Gogol, who may be very persuasively linked with Fonvizin. Leone Savoj, for example, points out that Fonvizin's correspondence of the 1760s with his family—in such things as its insistence upon his personal honesty and his difficulties in adjusting his personal relationships—exhibits remarkable parallels with Gogol's youthful correspondence with his mother. [3] The nineteenth-century scholar R. Sementkovsky also has remarked upon a considerable number of parallels between the lives and careers of the two men. [4]

In his extensive article of 1846 on the history of Russian literature entitled "What Is the Essence of Russian Poetry and What Are Its Peculiarities?" [5] Gogol allotted considerable space to Fonvizin, and especially to *The Minor*, in which he perceived only moral hideousness:

With horror you realize that you cannot influence [the negative characters in *The Minor*] either through the church or through the traditions of olden times of which they have retained only what is banal, and so only the iron of the law can have any impact upon them. Everything in this comedy seems to be a monstrous caricature on everything Russian. In reality, though, there is nothing of the caricature in it: all has been taken from the living reality of life and verified by the knowledge of the soul. These are the indisputable and hideous ideals of bestiality to which only a man of the Russian land, and not a member of any other nationality, can descend.[6]

As a playwright, Gogol resembled Fonvizin in many ways. Like Fonvizin he believed that art should depict not merely paradigms of evil but also exemplars of good. For that reason he set out to write his great novel *Dead Souls* in several parts. Although the first part, the only one completed, deals with the banality of Russian existence, Gogol intended to present his positive ideals in a later volume. Like Fonvizin, he hoped to improve public morality directly, through literature, and especially through the stage. His chosen instrument therefor was his finest comedy, *The Inspector-General* (1836), which describes the adventures of a native swindler who takes advantage of the greed of the officials in a provincial town. As in Gogol's interpretation of *The Minor*, there are no positive characters in this play: it was supposed to purge the evil qualities of humanity directly. Gogol was bitterly disappointed to discover that the social impact of his art fell short of his expectations, and left his native land for some time as a partial consequence. Fonvizin was by no means so unrealistic in his expectations as Gogol, but he evidently also hoped to purify the sink of public morality through the action of his art.

A brilliant student of Gogol, Alexander Slonimsky, has analyzed the serious effect of the comic in *The Minor*, the humorous underpinnings of Mrs. Prostakova's final tragedy, when, as he says, "Prostakova, a conventionally flat comic character, becomes psychologically more rounded and more complex because of the motif of genuine despair" after her son rejects her.[7] Slonimsky then points up the same tragic transformation at the end of *The Inspector-General*, when the mayor is transmogrified from a figure of fun into a desperate and hunted man. The final words of Gogol's play, Slonimsky points out, create a "starkly tragic impression"; like Starodum's concluding words in *The Minor*, they have the "ring of a moral sentence being passed."[8]

The Minor, *Woe from Wit*, and *The Inspector-General* all make serious social and moral points through the intrumentality of wit and humor. Vladimir Odoevsky, a leading intellectual of Pushkin's time and later, emphasized this point in a letter commenting on an early effort of the man who would almost single-handedly create the classical Russian theater of the nineteenth century, Alexander Ostrovsky. "I consider there to have been three tragedies in Russia," Odoevsky once wrote to a friend, "*The Minor, Woe from Wit*, and *The Inspector-General*. I would account [Ostrovsky's] *The Bankrupt* the fourth."[9] Ostrovsky has already left Fonvizin's more direct field of influence, but he resembles him in two major ways. In the first place, his plays concentrate upon the realistic depiction of Russian society—*byt*, to use the Russian term—and both *The Brigadier* and *The Minor* impressed contemporaries because they were so thoroughly rooted in contemporary social reality. Second, although he wrote relatively little, Fonvizin is remembered as the creator of the eighteenth-century Russian theater. Sumarokov wrote a much larger body of work for the theater than did Fonvizin, but somehow his plays were so divorced from the actual interests of society that they were soon forgotten. In a mirror-image of that, it fell to Ostrovsky—after the writing of brilliant individual plays by others— to provide the consistent substance of nineteenth-century Russian dramaturgy. In these senses he may be regarded as Fonvizin's heir.

One facet of Fedor Dostoevsky's work vividly illustrates the vitality of Fonvizin's influence many decades after his death. Dostoevsky's *Winter Notes on Summer Impressions* (1863), one of the more idiosyncratic works of Russian "travel" literature, written after Dostoevsky's first visit to Western Europe in 1862, is in part a dialogue with Fonvizin. Dostoevsky begins his second chapter with a quotation from Fonvizin's travel letters: "A Frenchman has no common sense [*rassudok*], and would consider it the greatest of misfortunes if he did."[10] That aphorism serves as a leitmotif for Dostoevsky's ruminations on Russia and Europe. Fonvizin, he remarks, must have been "tremendously pleased" with himself when he formulated it, and generations of Russians had since shared that satisfaction when they came across it.[11] Even the most ardent Russian Westernizers, Dostoevsky argued, were occasionally irritated at their cultural dependence, and deep down they applauded Fonvizin's act of intellectual defiance.

Dostoevsky begins the third chapter of *Winter Notes* with a brief essay on Fonvizin, who, he correctly says, was very much a product of Western culture. Although he "for some reason all his life wore a French-style coat, powder, and a sword sticking out behind him,"[12] when he went abroad he forthwith sought to set himself apart from that culture. And in this very reaction he was intensely Russian, Dostoevsky maintained. Dostoevsky dedicates another portion of the third chapter to a discussion of *The Brigadier*, the play in which Fonvizin dealt most directly with the cultural linkage between Russia and the West. Dostoevsky pays special attention to that episodic characte;, the wife-beater Gvozdilov, in whom he detects something "fundamental, elemental, and native."[13] Fonvizin evidently did not sympathize with Gvozdilov, but he still created him, and in so doing wrought better than he knew, Dostoevsky evidently thought.

The remainder of *Winter Notes* does not deal so directly with Fonvizin, but his slightly antiquarian presence still makes itself felt throughout. Dostoevsky even later refers again to the "Frenchman's common sense,"[14] and includes other, unacknowledged reminiscences of Fonvizin's travel letters as well—for example a reference to France as a "terrestrial paradise" which Dostoevsky utilizes as a partial basis for a philosophical digression far beyond anything in Fonvizin but still there present in embryo; and a passage in which Dostoevsky argues that Western "freedom" is merely a cloak for the oppression of the weak by the wealthy and powerful, which echoes Fonvizin's position and which was fairly widespread among Russian intellectuals of Dostoevsky's time.[15]

In the early 1860s Dostoevsky and his literary group worked out a philosophical view usually referred to as *pochvennichestvo*, emphasizing attachment to the native soil *(pochva)* and offered as a middle way between Westernism and Slavophilism. As we have seen, Fonvizin was in neither the proto-Slavophile nor the proto-Westernizer camp, and it may be that Dostoevsky sensed in him a forerunner of his own notions of the true relationship between Russia and the West, although there was no complete congruity in their views.[16]

Dostoevsky, along with Mikhail Saltykov-Shchedrin, was also one of the most powerful satirists of his time, another common bond between him and Fonvizin in the abstract. But the concrete reality with which the nineteenth-century satirists had to deal was so remote from that of Fonvizin's day that they could derive little assistance from his experience. Satire is, after all, rather topical, and great satirists have a more difficult time in speaking to generations following them by more than a century than great writers in other genres. The satire of a Dostoevsky, Saltykov-Shchedrin, or an Alexei Pisemsky was more bitter than humorous, and Fonvizin may very well have seemed too lighthearted to them.

In any case, Fonvizin did exert a vital influence on subsequent

Russian literature well into the nineteenth century. Even today he continues to be read with pleasure, at least when he can avoid the label of a high-school "classic." Undoubtedly he is one of the most fascinating figures in all the eighteenth century, and perhaps the most characteristic intellectual of Catherinian Russia.

Notes and References

Chapter One

1. Letter of first half of November 1824 to L. S. Pushkin, in Alexander Pushkin, *Polnoe sobranie sochinenii v desiati tomakh,* third edition (Moscow, 1966), X, 108.

2. See the account in Denis Fonvizin, *Chistoserdechnoe priznanie v delakh moikh i pomyshleniiakh,* in D. I. Fonvizin, *Sobranie sochinenii v dvukh tomakh* (Moscow-Leningrad, 1959), II, 83–84. Future references to this edition will be given in parentheses within the text.

3. For a summary of the controversy, see the extensive note 3 in K. V. Pigarev, *Tvorchestvo Fonvizina* (Moscow, 1954), pp. 290–91. In future this work will be referred to as Pigarev.

4. N. S. Tikhonravov, "D. I. Fon-Vizin," in *Sochineniia N. S. Tikhonravova* (Moscow, 1898), vol. III, part 1, pp. 90–91.

5. Letter to his parents of June 26, 1766, from Peterhof: II, 343.

6. "Mnenie o izbranii pies v 'Moskovskie sochineniia,' " II, 312–13.

7. A. S. Khvostov, "Poslanie k tvortsu poslaniia," published in the appendixes to P. A. Viazemskii, *Fon-Vizin,* in *Polnoe sobranie sochinenii kniazia P. A. Viazemskogo* (St. Petersburg, 1880), V, 219. This edition will hereafter be referred to as Viazemskii.

8. Much of the following is drawn from the excellent study by David Ransel, *The Politics of Catherinian Russia: The Panin Party* (New Haven and London, 1975).

9. *Ibid.,* p. 69.

10. See the listing in Fonvizin's letter of September 27, 1773, to Yakov Bulgakov, II, 398.

11. Viazemskii, pp. 158–59.

12. Viazemskii, p. 162.

13. The text of the petition is published in II, 611.

14. These memoirs are one of the best, though brief, sources on Fonvizin: "Fonvizin. Iz neizdannykh zapisok Klostermana," *Russkii arkhiv,* 1881, vol. III, book 2, pp. 291–99.

15. *Ibid.,* pp. 294–95.

16. Viazemskii, p. 161.

17. The text of the announcement is given as a lengthy footnote in II, 40–41.

18. See the letter of April 4, 1788, to Peter Panin, II, 499.

19. A partial reproduction of the announcement may be found in G. P. Makogonenko, *Denis Fonvizin: tvorcheskii put'* (Moscow-Leningrad, 1961), between pages 336 and 337.

20. Viazemskii, p. 168.

21. Letter to his sister of April 1766: II, 340–41.

22. I. I. Dmitriev, *Vzgliad na moiu zhizn'* (Moscow, 1866), pp. 58–60.

23. Ch. [Al. P. Chekhov], "Zabytaia istoricheskaia mogila," *Novoe vremia*, April 12, 1891, p. 2.

24. Miscellaneous notes by Mikhail Longinov in *Sovremennik*, No. 6, 1856, otd. V, p. 175.

Chapter Two

1. R. Sementkovskii, "Nash pervyi skeptik," *Istoricheskii vestnik*, No. 7 (July 1895): 117.

2. For a discussion of the "Epistle," see the chapter in Hildegard Schroeder, *Russische Verssatire im 18. Jahrhundert* (Cologne and Graz, 1962), pp. 168–71.

3. On this topic, see N. Lavrovskii, "K biografii Fon-Vizina," *Zhurnal Ministerstva narodnogo prosveshcheniia*, No. 4 (April 1872): 208–19.

4. See especially Aleksei Stankevich, "*Al'zira* Vol'tera v perevode Fon-Vizina," *Russkii arkhiv*, No. 10 (1887): 304–12.

5. A. Strycek, *Denis Fonvizine* (Paris, 1976), pp. 92–94. Cited hereafter as Strycek.

6. A good discussion of the *Fables* is to be found in chapter 6 of Strycek, pp. 56–63.

7. N.S. Tikhonravov, "D. I. Fon-Vizin," in *Sochineniia N. S. Tikhonravova* (Moscow, 1898), vol. III, part 1, p. 104.

8. Viazemskii, p. 35.

9. Dmitriev, *Vzgliad na moiu zhizn'*, p. 85.

10. In his small book *D. I. Fonvizin* (Moscow, 1945), Dmitry Blagoy refers several times to connections between Kantemir and Fonvizin, but no specialized study of them has ever been done.

11. Strycek dedicates the entire third part of his book (pp, 205–316) to a discussion of numerous contributions to Novikov's satirical journals of 1769–73 which he attributes to Fonvizin on the basis of internal, and particularly stylistic, evidence. These contributions do express ideas more or less congruent with Fonvizin's, but the internal evidence seems to me too feeble a reed upon which to base a definite attribution. In addition, between 1770 and 1777, except for the brief brochure on the Grand Duke Paul's recovery, he published nothing which we may ascribe to him with certainty. It seems likely that Fonvizin was so occupied with his official duties during this time of turmoil that he had little time even to write the brief pieces

published in Novikov's journals. He *may* have been the author of some or all the works which Strycek singles out, but his authorship is far from proven.

Chapter Three

1. That is K.V. Pigarev's considered opinion, for instance: Pigarev, p. 91.
2. D. Blagoi, *D. I. Fonvizin* (Moscow, 1945), p. 81.
3. V.G. Belinskii, "Sochineniia Aleksandra Pushkina. Stat'ia pervaia," in V.G. Belinskii, *Estetika i literaturnaia kritika v dvukh tomakh* (Moscow, 1959), II, 149. It should also be noted that Belinsky had a low opinion of Molière.
4. [S.S. Dudyshkin], Review of Fonvizin's *Sochineniia* in the Smirdin edition of 1846, *Otechestvennye zapiski*, No. 9, 1847, otd. V, p. 42.
5. M.M. Kheraskov, "K satiricheskoi muze," *Izbrannye proizvedeniia* (Leningrad, 1961), pp. 103–105.
6. See N.S. Tikhonravov, "D. I. Fon-Vizin," in *Sochineniia N.S. Tikhonravova* (Moscow, 1898), vol. III, part 1, p. 103.
7. This is one of several good points made in David J. Welsh's useful *Russian Comedy 1765–1823* (The Hague and Paris, 1966), pp. 32–33.
8. A. Shakhovskoi, "Predislovie k Polubarskim zateiam," *Syn Otechestva*, vol. 61, 1820, pp. 11–26.
9. Grigorii Gukovskii, "Vokrug Radishcheva," in Gukovskii, *Ocherki po istorii russkoi literatury i obshschestvennoi mysli XVIII veka* (Leningrad, 1938), p. 185.
10. L.G. Barag, "Komediia Fonvizina 'Nedorosl' ' i russkaia literatura kontsa XVIII veka," in *Problemy realizma v russkoi literature XVIII veka: Sbornik statei* (Moscow-Leningrad, 1940), p. 110.
11. Gukovskii, *op cit.*, p. 182.
12. Strycek, pp. 153–54.
13. Shakhovskoi, *op cit.*, pp. 24–25.
14. Novikov referred to it thus in his *Opyt istoricheskogo slovaria o rossiiskikh pisateliakh* of 1772: see, e.g., the partial publication in A.D. Orishin, ed., *Khrestomatiia kriticheskikh materialov po russkoi literature XVIII veka* (Lvov, 1959), p. 118.
15. Welsh, *Russian Comedy*, p. 104.
16. *Zimnie zametki o letnikh vpechatleniiakh* (1863), in F. M. Dostoevskii, *Sobranie sochinenii* (Moscow, 1956), IV, 77–78.
17. See "O Brigadire Fonvizina," in N.G.Chernyshevskii, *Polnoe sobranie sochinenii v 15-i tomakh* (Moscow, 1949), II, 798–99, 801.
18. Marvin Kantor, "Writings," in Marvin Kantor, ed., *Dramatic Works of D.I. Fonvizin* (Frankfurt/Main, 1974), p. 32. See also Kantor's "Fonvizin and Holberg: A Comparison of *The Brigadier* and *Jean de France*," *Canadian Slavic Studies*, VII, 4 (1973): 475–84.
19. Chernyshevskii, *op cit.*, pp. 804–805.

Chapter Four

1. See, for example, Strycek, pp. 370–71.

2. A. P. Mogilianskii, "K voprosu o tak nazyvaemom 'rannem' *Nedorosle," XVIII vek*, No. 4 (1959): 415–21.

3. See "Prilozhenie II. O tak nazyvaemoi rannei redaktsii *Nedoroslia*,*" in Pigarev, pp. 281–84.

4. Quoted in Pigarev, p. 151.

5. For a fragmentary stage history of the play, see the article by B. Varneke, *"Nedorosl'* na stsene," in Iu. E. Ozarovskii, ed., *P'esy khudozhestvennogo repertuara i postanovka ikh na stsene. Vypusk I. Nedorosl'* (St. Petersburg, 1901), pp. 140–47.

6. P.N. Berkov, "Teatr Fonvizina i russkaia kul'tura," in *Russkie klassiki i teatr* (Moscow-Leningrad, 1947), pp. 86–87.

7. For information on Maddox, see K.A. Papmehl, *Freedom of Expression in Eighteenth Century Russia* (The Hague, 1971), p. 105n.

8. E. Kheksel'shnaider, "O pervom nemetskom perevode *Nedoroslia* Fonvizina," *XVIII vek*, No. 4 (1959): 334–38.

9. V.V. Sipovskii, "Iz istorii russkoi komedii XVIII veka," in Akademiia nauk, *Izvestiia Otdeleniia russkogo iazyka i slovesnosti*, XXII, 1 (1917): 205–74.

10. L.G. Barag, "Komediia Fonvizina *Nedorosl'* i russkaia literatura kontsa XVIII veka," in *Problemy realizma v russkoi literature XVIII veka: Sbornik statei* (Moscow-Leningrad, 1940), pp. 113–20.

11. Pigarev, p. 211.

12. Viazemskii, p. 133. In this particular instance Vyazemsky was speaking of *The Brigadier*, but the sentiment applies equally well to *The Minor*.

13. L. I. Kulakova, *Denis Ivanovich Fonvizin* (Moscow-Leningrad, 1966), p. 108. Kulakova does not indicate the source of her information.

14. V.O. Kliuchevskii, "Nedorosl' Fonvizina (Opyt istoricheskogo ob"iasneniia uchebnoi p'esy)," in Kliuchevskii, *Sochineniia* (Moscow, 1959), VIII, 263–87.

15. Pigarev, p. 197.

16. Berkov, "Teatr Fonvizina i russkaia kul'tura," p. 77.

17. Viazemskii, p. 136.

18. Berkov, "Teatr Fonvizina i russkaia kul'tura," p. 75.

19. See I. Zhdanov's article on Fonvizin in the *Russkii biograficheskii slovar'* (St. Petersburg, 1901), XXI, 184.

20. David Patterson, "Fonvizin's *Nedorosl'* as a Russian Representative of the *Genre sérieux*," *Comparative Literature Studies*, XIV, 3 (September 1977): 196–204.

21. Kulakova, *Fonvizin*, pp. 96–97.

22. Marvin Kantor, "Writings," in *Dramatic Works of D. I. Fonvizin* (Frankfurt/Main, 1974), p. 38.

23. G. Gukovskii, "Problemy stsenicheskogo voploshcheniia *Nedoroslia*

Fonvizina," in *Teatral'nyi al'manakh: Sbornik statei i materialov*, No. 1 (1946): 153–70.

24. Viazemskii, p. 139.
25. Welsh, *Russian Comedy*, p. 67. Welsh presents a good summary of the tradition of the *raisonneur* here, pp. 66–69.
26. See Dmitri Strémooukhoff, "Autour du *Nedorosl'* de Fonvizin," *Revue des études slaves*, No. 38, 1961, pp. 189–91. A small selection of Dmitriev-Mamonov's writings has been published in *Poety XVIII veka*, second edition (Leningrad, 1972), I, 429–50.

Chapter Five

1. Discussions of the travel letters may be found in: Hans Rogger, *National Consciousness in Eighteenth Century Russia* (Cambridge, Mass., 1960), pp. 75–84; and Reuel K. Wilson, *The Literary Travelogue: A Comparative Study with Special Relevance to Russian Literature from Fonvizin to Pushkin* (The Hague, 1973), pp. 31–38.
2. Pigarev, p. 131.
3. N.S. Tikhonravov, "D. I. Fonvizin," in *Sochineniia N.S. Tikhonravova* (Moscow, 1898), vol. III, part 1, p. 120.
4. "Vzgliad na russkuiu literaturu so smerti Pushkina," in Apollon Grigor'ev, *Literaturnaia kritika* (Moscow, 1967), p. 171.
5. Leone Savoj, *Saggio di nuna biografia del Fon-Vizin* (Rome, 1935), p. 73.
6. Viazemskii, pp. 75, 80.
7. *Ibid.*, pp. 87–88.
8. Strycek, pp. 359–61.
9. *Ibid.*, pp. 361–62, 473–75.
10. See V.V. Sipovskii, *N.M. Karamzin, avtor "Pisem russkogo puteshestvennika"* (St. Petersburg, 1899), pp. 238–362.
11. Welsh, *Russian Comedy*, pp. 49–50.
12. Chapter on Fonvizin in G.V. Plekhanov, *Istoriia russkoi obshchestvennoi mysli* (Moscow-Leningrad, 1925), III, 93.

Chapter Six

1. Ransel, *The Politics of Catherinian Russia*, p. 21.
2. Ransel, p. 11.
3. *Ibid.*, p. 92. Cf. the entire section here on the "Imperial Council Reform," pp. 84–92.
4. Papmehl, *Freedom of Expression*, pp. 84–85.
5. *Ibid.*, pp. 86–87.
6. In *The Politics of Catherinian Russia* (pp. 269–77), Ransel offers a good general summary of what he terms "Starodumstvo," or the Fonvizinian variant of the Panin party's program as he interprets it.

7. Ransel, p. 183 n43.
8. *Ibid.*, p. 193.
9. Walter Gleason, "Changes in Values among Certain Russian Writers of the 1760s," unpublished diss., University of Chicago, 1973, pp. 69, 137.
10. Vladimir Nabokov, trans. and ed., *Eugene Onegin: A Novel in Verse by Aleksandr Pushkin* (New York, 1964), II, 82.
11. L. A. Kulakova, "Kogda napisana basnia 'Lisitsa-Kaznodei'?" in *Rol' i znachenie literatury XVIII veka v istorii russkoi kul'tury (XVIII vek,* No. 7, Moscow-Leningrad, 1966), pp. 174–80.

Chapter Seven

1. Viazemskii, p. 19.
2. *Ibid.*, pp. 189–90.
3. V. Istomin, "Glavneishie osobennosti iazyka i sloga proizvedenii D. I. Fonvizina. 1744–1792," *Russkii filologicheskii vestnik*, No. 3–4, 1897, section II, pp. 1–33.
4. K. P. Petrov, *Slovar' k sochineniiam i perevodam D. I. Fon-Vizina* (St. Petersburg, 1904).
5. See the article on Elagin in the Brokgauz-Efron encyclopedia.
6. N. S. Tikhonravov, "D. I. Fon-Vizin," *Sochineniia N. S. Tikhonravova* (Moscow, 1898), vol. III, part 1, p. 109.
7. Strycek, pp. 401–404. See also Pigarev, p. 187.
8. Gukovskii, "Vokrug Radishcheva," p. 191.
9. See the chapter "Fonvizin" in M. I. Sukhomlinov, *Istoriia Rossiiskoi akademii* (St. Petersburg, 1885), VII, 10–22; and also the chapter on the dictionaries of the Russian Academy in Ralia Tseitlin, *Kratkii ocherk istorii russkoi leksikografii (slovari russkogo iazyka)* (Moscow, 1958), pp. 27–33.
10. *Ibid.*, p. 29.
11. Strycek, p. 429.

Chapter Eight

1. *Ten' Fonvizina*, in A. Pushkin, *Polnoe sobranie sochinenii v desiati tomakh* (Moscow, 1962), third edition, I, 164.
2. *Ibid.*, V, 547.
3. Leone Savoj, *Saggio di una biografia del Fon-Vizin* (Rome, 1935), pp. 26–27.
4. See R. Sementkovskii, "Nash pervyi skeptik," *Istoricheskii vestnik*, No. 7 (July 1895), pp. 112–33 *passim*.
5. "V chem zhe, nakonets, sushchestvo russkoi poezii i v chem ee osobennost'?" (1846), in N. V. Gogol', *Sobranie sochinenii v semi tomakh* (Moscow, 1967), VI, 159–203.
6. *Ibid.*, p. 190.
7. Alexander Slonimsky, "The Technique of the Comic in Gogol," in

Robert A. Maguire, ed., *Gogol from the Twentieth Century* (Princeton, 1974), p. 328.

8. *Ibid.*, pp. 328–29.

9. S. V. Maksimov, "Aleksandr Nikolaevich Ostrovskii," in *A. N. Ostrovskii v vospominaniiakh sovremennikov* (Moscow, 1966), p. 90.

10. F. M. Dostoevskii, *Sobranie sochinenii* (Moscow, 1956), IV, 66.

11. *Ibid.*, pp. 66–67.

12. *Ibid.*, p. 71.

13. *Ibid.*, p. 78.

14. *Ibid.*, pp. 85, 88.

15. *Ibid.*, pp. 101, 105.

16. For a treatment of the connections between the two authors, see G. M. Fridlender, "Dostoevskii i Fonvizin," *Russkaia literatura XVIII veka i ee mezhdunarodnye sviazi* (*XVIII vek*, No. 10, Leningrad, 1975), pp. 92–97.

Selected Bibliography

PRIMARY SOURCES

1. Editions of Fonvizin's Works in Russian

Nedorosl'. Komediia v 5-ti deistviiakh. St. Petersburg: Shnor, 1783.

Polnoe sobranie sochinenii. P. P. Beketov, ed. In four parts. Moscow: I. G. Salaev, 1830.

Sochineniia, pis'ma i izbrannye perevody. P. A. Efremov, ed. St. Petersburg: I. I. Glazunov, 1866. The most authoritative prerevolutionary edition.

Pervoe polnoe sobranie sochinenii, kak original'nykh, tak i perevodnykh. St. Petersburg and Moscow: K. K. Shamov, 1888.

Sochineniia. A. I. Vvedenskii, ed. St. Petersburg: A. F. Marks, 1893.

Sobranie sochinenii. G. P. Makogonenko, ed. Moscow-Leningrad: Goslitizdat, 1959. 2 vols. The standard modern edition.

2. Translations of Fonvizin's Writings into English

The Minor

The Young Hopeful. Trans. George R. Noyes and George Z. Patrick, in George R. Noyes, ed., *Masterpieces of the Russian Drama.* New York: Dover Publications, 1961 (originally published 1933), I, 27–84.

The Minor. Trans. Frank D. Reeve, in Frank Reeve, ed., *An Anthology of Russian Plays.* New York: Vintage, 1961, I, 21–83.

The Minor. Trans. Marvin Kantor, in Marvin Kantor, ed., *Dramatic Works of D. I. Fonvizin.* Bern: Herbert Lang, and Frankfurt/Main: Peter Lang, 1974, pp. 87–134.

The Brigadier

The Brigadier. In Harold B. Segel, ed., *The Literature of Eighteenth-Century Russia: A History and Anthology.* New York: Dutton, 1967, II, 321–73.

The Brigadier. Trans. Marvin Kantor, in Kantor, *Dramatic Works of Fonvizin,* pp. 49–86.

The Selection of a Tutor

The Choice of a Tutor. In Carl E. B. Roberts, ed., *Five Russian Plays with One from Ukrainian.* New York: Dutton, 1916, pp. 79–99.

The Selection of a Tutor. Trans. Marvin Kantor, in Kantor, *Dramatic Works of Fonvizin,* pp. 141–50.

Travel Letters

"Letters to Count P. I. Panin During His First Journey Abroad (Excerpts)," in Leo Wiener, ed., *Anthology of Russian Literature*. New York: Putnam, 1902, I, 355–58.

"Letters from My Second Journey Abroad," "Letters from My Third Journey Abroad," in Segel, *The Literature of Eighteenth-Century Russia*, I, 304–51.

Ta-Gio

"Ta Hsüeh, Or That Great Learning Which Comprises Higher Chinese Philosophy." Trans. Ronald Hingley, in Marc Raeff, ed., *Russian Intellectual History: An Anthology*. New York: Harcourt, Brace and World, 1966, pp. 88–95.

A Discourse on Permanent Laws of the State

"A Discourse on Permanent Laws of the State." Trans. Ronald Hingley, in Raeff, *Russian Intellectual History*, pp. 96–105.

Universal Courtiers Grammar

"Universal Courtiers Grammar." Trans. Bernard G. Guerney, in Bernard G. Guerney, ed., *The Portable Russian Reader*. New York: Viking, 1947, pp. 23–27.

An Open-Hearted Confession

"An Open-Hearted Confession (Excerpts)." Trans. Leo Wiener, in Wiener, *Anthology of Russian Literature*, I, 351–55.

SECONDARY SOURCES

BARAG, L. G. "Komediia Fonvizina *Nedorosl'* i russkaia literatura kontsa XVIII veka," in N. K. Gudzii, ed., *Problemy realizma v russkoi literature XVIII veka: Sbornik statei*. Moscow: Izdatel'stvo Akademii nauk SSSR, 1940, pp. 68–120. A general article on *The Minor*, most useful in placing the play in the context of its time and in tracing its influence on now-forgotten theatrical works of the quarter-century after its publication.

BERKOV, PAVEL. "Teatr Fonvizina i russkaia kul'tura," in *Russkie klassiki i teatr*. Leningrad: Iskusstvo, 1947, pp. 7–108. A wide-ranging article which deals with Fonvizin's plays in detail and sets them in the context of the history of Russian theater of the period.

BLAGOI, DMITRII. *D. I. Fonvizin*. Moscow: Gosudarstvennoe izdatel'stvo khudozhestvennoi literatury, 1945. A small volume of a general nature by a leading Soviet specialist on Russian literature of the eighteenth century. Despite its brevity and doctrinal orthodoxy, contains some stimulating passages on more general problems connected with Fonvizin's life and work.

KANTOR, MARVIN. "Life," "Writings," in Marvin Kantor, ed., *Dramatic Works of D. I. Fonvizin*. Bern: Herbert Lang, and Frankfurt/Main: Peter Lang, 1974, pp. 11–24, 25–45. The pioneering treatment of Fonvizin's life and works in English. Provides a good overview of the subject.

KLIUCHEVSKII, VASILII. "Nedorosl' Fonvizina (Opyt istoricheskogo ob" ias-neniia uchebnoi p'esy)," in V. O. Kliuchevskii, *Sochineniia*. Moscow: Gosudarstevennoe izdatel'stvo politicheskoi literatury, 1959, VIII, 263–87. As opinionated as almost all of this famous historian's writing, this well-known article discusses *The Minor* as a source of historical information. More valuable as a key to Klyuchevsky's mind than Fonvizin's.

KULAKOVA, L. I. *Denis Ivanovich Fonvizin*. Moscow-Leningrad: Pros-veshchenie, 1966. Brief and without scholarly apparatus, but judicious in its conclusions for a Soviet work, and even quite stimulating in places.

MAKOGONENKO, GEORGII. *Denis Fonvizin: Tvorcheskii put'*. Moscow-Leningrad: Gosudarstvennyi izdatel'stvo khudozhestvennoi literatury, 1961. A detailed discussion of many aspects of Fonvizin's life and work by a leading Soviet specialist in the period. Makogonenko is good at unearthing new material in the history of that time, but not very inspiring in his interpretations of that material.

PIGAREV, KIRIL. *Tvorchestvo Fonvizina*. Moscow: Izdatel'stvo Akademii nauk SSSR, 1954. The most thorough, judicious, and scholarly study of Fonvizin in Russian. Indispensable for the serious student of Fonvizin.

SAVOJ, LEONE. *Saggio di una biografia del Fon-Vizin*. Rome: Istituto per l'Europa orientale, 1935. A short book containing a series of studies of Fonvizin's life and work from beginning to end, but with heavy emphasis on the period of the 1760s and his personal psychology as illuminated by his correspondence of that time. Rather spotty for later decades.

STRYCEK, ALEXIS. *Denis Fonvizine*. Paris: Librairie des cinq continents, 1976. The first highly detailed study of Fonvizin to have appeared in a Western language. Pays scrupulous attention to everything, including especially Western influences in his writing. So thorough that it is more helpful as a reference work on Fonvizin than as an introduction to him.

VIAZEMSKII, PETR. *Fon-Vizin*, in Viazemskii, *Polnoe sobranie sochinenii*. St. Petersburg: Izdatel'stvo grafa S. D. Sheremeteva, 1880, volume 5 (originally published in 1848). One of the few early nineteenth-century studies of an eighteenth-century author still frequently used, in part because Vyazemsky had access not only to people but also to documents which have since disappeared. Vyazemsky's interpretations tend to be idiosyncratic.

Index